IMAGES
of America

GRAPEVINE

When the historic 1901 Cotton Belt Railroad Depot closed in 1972, the Grapevine Garden Club saved it from destruction and formed the Grapevine Historical Society. The old depot became symbolic of the mission to preserve the community's history and is the home of the Grapevine Historical Museum. The artifacts in the museum have been donated by local people and include things from prehistoric times, such as fossils and dinosaur tracks to mid-20th-century women's fashions. Each year, thousands of visitors from all over the world examine 19th-century home and farm implements, antique typewriters, wedding dresses, and photographs of the early Grape Vine Prairie settlers. The depot was returned to its original site at the Grapevine Heritage Center in 1992. In 2010, the Grapevine Historical Society is planning to move the museum to a renovated building on Hudgins Street. (Courtesy of the Grapevine Historical Society.)

ON THE COVER: The railroad is coming! With its proximity to two major economic centers, Grape Vine was destined to have a railroad. In 1888, the St. Louis Southwestern Railroad, otherwise known as the Cotton Belt Railroad, steamed into town. Grape Vine began to thrive as an agricultural trade center supplying goods to the area's farmers and serving as a shipping point for their produce. Captured in this 1907 photograph are farmers and businessmen waiting for the arrival of the train. (Courtesy of the Grapevine Historical Society.)

IMAGES
of America

GRAPEVINE

The Grapevine Historical Society with
Joe Ann Standlee and Margaret Rains Harper

ARCADIA
PUBLISHING

Library of Congress Control Number: 2010925222

For all general information contact Arcadia Publishing at:
Telephone 843-853-2070
Fax 843-853-0044
E-mail sales@arcadiapublishing.com
For customer service and orders:
Toll-Free 1-888-313-2665

Visit us on the Internet at www.arcadiapublishing.com

*This book is dedicated to Mary Virginia Wall Simmons
who loved Grapevine, its people, and its history. Her roots
began here, and her legacy moves into the future.*

CONTENTS

ACKNOWLEDGMENTS

We would like to thank the Grapevine Historical Society for entrusting us with the task of providing a pictorial history of Grapevine and the Grapevine Historical Society Executive Board for their support and encouragement. Without the works of so many diligent historians who have come before us in researching, writing, and photographing Grapevine's rich history, this would have been an insurmountable task. Special thanks to the Grapevine Historical Society, who sponsored and published *Grapevine Area History* and *Grapevine Area History Supplement, 1979–1989,* and to Charles H. Young, the editor of those books, who left a legacy for others to follow. Also thank you to book coordinator Sandra Tate and her committee from the Grapevine Historical Society for compiling stories in *Grapevine's Most Unforgettable Characters* in 2006. These sources are full of invaluable information and local color.

The Grapevine Historic Preservation Commission, the Grapevine Heritage Foundation, and the Grapevine Convention and Visitors Bureau have given us counsel and access to their files. The following individuals have given time and talent to accurately tell Grapevine's story: Carolyn and Paul Ernst, Sallie Andrews, Ken Slade, David Klempin, Josh Tate, Charles D. Young, Dr. Ed Lancaster, Tim Lancaster, Judy Deacon Jacobs, Helen Jean Lucas Reed, Harlan Jewett, Bruce A. Standlee, Margaret Telford, Balla and Joe Wright, Debi Meek, J. E. Foust III, Janet Willhoite Dickey, Janis Roberson, Susan Jackson, Tom Simmons, Gayle Hall, Dianne and Jerry Pair, Bill Powers, Jessie Lou Nelson, Paul W. McCallum, Ross Bannister, Pamela L. Price, Janie Harper, Stephanie Harper Lucke, Rebeka Cook, Dan Truex, Vivian Tribble, Sandra Tate, Ralph Gary, Margaret Wood, Archie St. Clair, Lt. Todd Dearing, Marcy Roitman Boothe, Duane Gage, the Scott Hardeman Family, Keith Miller, Marsha Stephenson, Nancy Norris, Darlene Freed, Deby Miller, Joe Moore, and others we may have failed to mention. A special thanks goes to those at the city offices of Grapevine who have taken our many calls and answered our endless questions and e-mails and have given us access to their files and Web sites.

Our editors at Arcadia, Kristie Kelly and Hannah Carney, have given us encouragement, wisdom, and expert editing, and we appreciate their kindness.

We owe our husbands, Bill Standlee and Tim Harper, a great deal of gratitude and thanks for their encouragement and support and for withstanding perhaps a bit of neglect during the production process.

> Joe Ann Standlee and Margaret Rains Harper
> Book Coordinators, Grapevine Historical Society
> To God be the Glory!

INTRODUCTION

Archeological evidence indicates the presence of humans around Grape Vine Springs for at least the past 10,000 to 12,000 years. Scholars believe that in the 1300s, Caddoan peoples roamed here in their hunting and gathering expeditions. The early-19th-century pioneers, therefore, were not the first people to occupy this rich prairie land, but by the time they arrived, most of the Native Americans had moved on. In 1843, Sam Houston and representatives of the Republic of Texas came to Grape Vine Springs to make peace with those tribes left in the area, but the Native Americans never made it to the meeting. Later that same year, the natives and Gen. Edward H. Tarrant, for whom Tarrant County was named, finalized a treaty of peace and friendship at Bird's Fort. This document opened North Texas for settlement.

The first settlers began to arrive on the Grape Vine Prairie in the 1840s, including families from the Peters Colony and the Missouri Colony. Community leaders met in 1854 for the purpose of laying out the original township and arranging for a post office. A discussion ensued over the town's name, since Grapevine had been called Leonardsville and later Dunnsville, after two pioneer families. The dispute was taken to Judge James Tracy Morehead, who recommended the name "Grape Vine" because of the prolific wild mustang grapes so abundant in the area and the proximity to the springs and prairie of the same name. On January 12, 1914, the U.S. Postal Service changed the name to "Grapevine," and it is now recognized as the first permanent settlement in Tarrant County, preceding Fort Worth by several years.

When the Civil War broke out, the citizens of Grape Vine contributed more than their share of Confederate soldiers to defend the South. One hundred men volunteered with a unit called the Grape Vine Mounted Rangers, and the ladies of Grape Vine made them a "flag of our country," as it was called by Martha Moorehead Quayle in her speech for presentation in August 1861, to remind them that they were protecting their families. Although many were reluctant to leave Texas and fight in the East, the soldiers fought valiantly to protect their homes from Yankee invasion. One of the few Texans to achieve the rank of general in the Confederate Army was Dr. Richard Gano from Grape Vine, who was also the Tarrant County representative in the state legislature.

Grape Vine benefited from the great industrial expansion in the 1870s and 1880s with the invention of the modern plows used on the black soil of Grape Vine Prairie and, in 1888, by the arrival of the Cotton Belt Railroad. Duane Gage, a history professor at Tarrant County College, explains the railroad's influence on Grapevine: "The farming village—which might have faded away like many other rural villages that were bypassed—began to thrive as an agricultural trade center." As a result, the Wallis Hotel joined the 1870s Baker Hotel to serve the travelers, and in 1900, the first rural telephone was installed, and many of the brick buildings on Main Street were constructed. At this time, the town had a population of 500. In 1902, the Farmers and Merchants Milling Company was organized, later to become B&D Mills. The farming community was on its way to supplying cotton, corn, grains, truck farm crops, meat, and dairy products to the Dallas and Fort Worth region and beyond.

During World War I and World War II, the citizens of Grapevine supported the war efforts, and many young men and women went to war. The following quotation is taken from an article found in the *Grapevine Sun* on November 3, 1942: "There will be a drive here in Grapevine to show that Grapevine is all out for the War Effort. Grapevine and community are represented in all branches of the service on all parts of the globe. The least we can possibly do is to sustain the efforts of these brave men."

The infamous Bonnie Parker and Clyde Barrow Gang was active around the Grapevine area. In 1932, the Grapevine Home Bank was robbed by J. Les "Red" Stewart and Odell Chambless, colleagues of Bonnie and Clyde. Bonnie and Clyde killed two state highway patrolmen at State Highway 114 and Dove Road in 1934. A historical marker locates this spot today. Bonnie and Clyde were later tracked down and killed in Louisiana in the same year, thus ending their reign of terror.

In 1947, flood control became an important issue in the region, and the U.S. Army Corps of Engineers began building a dam 1 mile northeast of Grapevine. Work was completed in 1952, and Lake Grapevine was created. It not only helped with flood control but also furnished a water supply for Grapevine, Dallas, and several other municipalities. The lake became popular as a source of recreation for boaters, fishermen, and vacationers and helped the community of 1,824 in 1950 grow to 2,823 by 1960.

Another major development, begun in 1965, pushed the city of Grapevine into the limelight of the Dallas-Fort Worth Metroplex. These two cities initiated a project to build the nation's largest regional airport at that time on the Grape Vine Prairie in 1985. It would become the Dallas-Fort Worth International Airport. When dust had settled and the Dallas-Fort Worth Regional Airport opened on January 13, 1974, two-thirds of it was located within the city limits of Grapevine, just south of the downtown area. By 1980, the population of Grapevine had grown to 11,801.

In 1972, the Cotton Belt Railroad closed the Grapevine depot for business. However, some enterprising historians in the Grapevine Garden Club stepped forward to save it from destruction and ultimately formed the Grapevine Historical Society. Out of this event came the impetus to protect the growing community from the urbanization that often destroys the history of a fast-growing area. The people of Grapevine began donating items of historical significance, and a fine little museum was established in the depot. When it became known that an old log cabin, built in 1845 on Dove Road and eventually occupied by the Torian family, was to be destroyed, the historical society set about to save it and had it moved to Main Street in 1976. The Torian Cabin now stands as a tribute to the pioneer spirit that built the community as well as to those who seek to preserve it.

In 1984, Grapevine became a member of the Texas Main Street Program, and in 1986, the Main Street merchants constructed the Gazebo. Interest in preserving and revitalizing this thoroughfare became high priority to the community leaders. In 1991, the City of Grapevine adopted a historic preservation ordinance in an effort to protect the city's architectural heritage and, along with the Grapevine Heritage Foundation, has preserved the 1940s art deco Palace Theatre downtown on Main Street. They also restored the *c.* 1859 Thomas Jefferson Nash Farm, the oldest intact farmstead in Tarrant County, to reflect the life and times of early Grapevine farmers and settlers.

Grapevine's storied past and the progressive thinking of its city leaders have caused it to rank among the top cities to visit in Texas. According to the Grapevine Historical Society Museum's visitor log, this quaint little prairie town has now gained attention from people all over the world.

One

GRAPEVINE

A DOOR TO THE WORLD

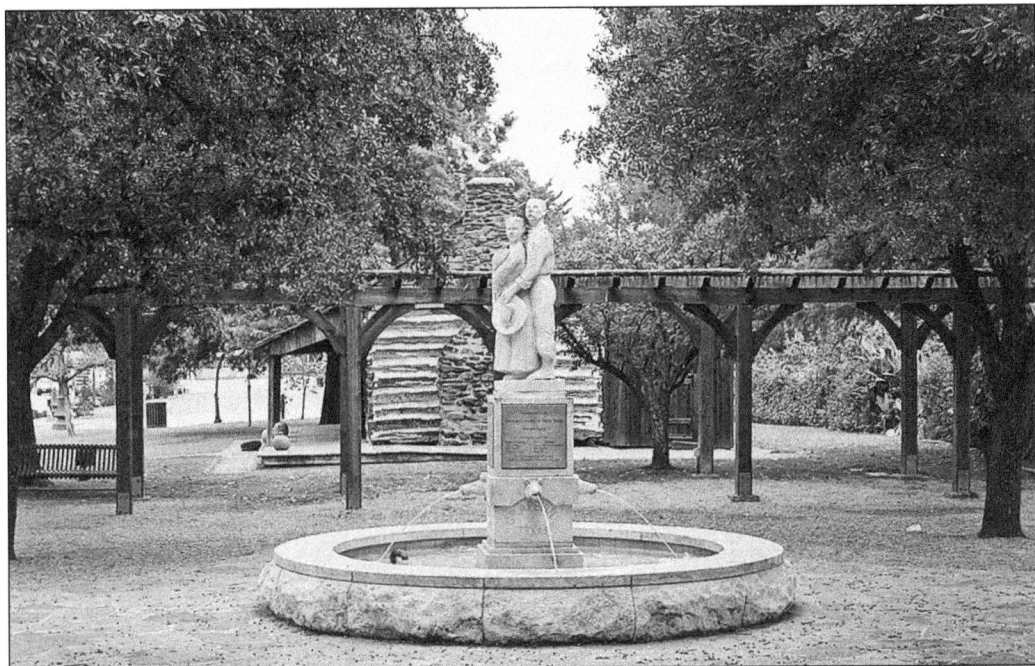

Walking To Texas, created by Michael Cunningham, is a sculpture in honor of the pioneer families who came to the Grape Vine Prairie seeking opportunity and a new life. The baby in the arms of the mother and the protective embrace of the father show family strength and unity as they gaze unafraid into the future. Located in Liberty Park Plaza on Main Street, it was Grapevine's first piece of public art and was dedicated in December 1996.

THE PETERS COLONY
IN TARRANT COUNTY

IN 1841, W. S. PETERS OF KENTUCKY
AND ASSOCIATES CONTRACTED WITH
THE REPUBLIC OF TEXAS TO BRING
IMMIGRANTS TO THIS AREA. BY 1848,
PETERS COLONY LAND COVERED
NEARLY 2 MILLION ACRES IN NORTH
CENTRAL TEXAS, INCLUDING ALL OF
TARRANT COUNTY. SPECULATION IN
UNLOCATED LAND CERTIFICATES WAS
RAMPANT. ABOUT 150 COLONISTS AND
THEIR FAMILIES, MOST OF WHOM
WERE AMERICAN-BORN FARMERS OF
MEAGER MEANS, SETTLED IN TARRANT
COUNTY. AS THE MOST EXTENSIVE
EMPRESARIO ENTERPRISE UNDERTAKEN
BY THE REPUBLIC, THE PETERS COLONY
HELPED OPEN THIS AREA OF TEXAS
TO SETTLEMENT.

(1985, 1990)

On August 30, 1841, W. S. Peters of Kentucky and 19 associates entered into a contract with the Republic of Texas to bring badly needed emigrants into this area. By 1848, their land covered nearly 2 million acres in North Central Texas, including all of Tarrant County and what is now the city of Grapevine.

10

THE MISSOURI COLONY

IN 1844 RELATED FAMILIES FROM PLATTE COUNTY, MISSOURI, SETTLED IN THIS AREA. JAMES GIBSON, ONE OF THE EARLIEST SETTLERS IN TARRANT COUNTY, OWNED THIS SITE. IN 1845 MORE RELATIVES AND FRIENDS ARRIVED. THEY BECAME KNOWN AS THE "MISSOURI COLONY". THE PIONEERS RAISED CATTLE AND GRAIN. JOHN A. FREEMAN TAUGHT SCHOOL AND PREACHED TO THE SETTLERS AT LONESOME DOVE. SOME ORIGINAL COLONISTS MOVED TO PIONEER OTHER FRONTIER REGIONS. OTHERS REMAINED TO HELP BUILD THE NORTHEASTERN SECTION OF TARRANT COUNTY, THE FIRST PERMANENTLY SETTLED AREA IN THE COUNTY.

(1979)

Several closely related families from Platte County, Missouri, settled on the Grape Vine Prairie in 1844. The pioneers became known as the "Missouri Colony." Rev. John Allen Freeman taught school and preached to the settlers at Lonesome Dove.

The oil painting, *Walking to Texas*, shows a long line of pioneers as they entered the Grape Vine Prairie. These families endured the long journey on foot, in covered wagons, and on horseback, slowly advancing along the sun-drenched trail to Texas, a promising new place of opportunity they would soon call home. Anthony Gail "Tony" Eubanks, a Grapevine resident, was commissioned by the City of Grapevine to create this oil painting, located in city hall.

This wagon wheel came from the covered wagon of Rev. Daniel Starr, who made the trip from Illinois to Grape Vine in 1854. Around 1887, in order to feed the railroad construction crews, the wheel was used as a reel to lift up beef carcasses during the butchering process.

In 1854, the settlers drew up plans for the original township and applied for a U.S. post office. A dispute ensued over the town's official name, since Grapevine was originally called Leonardsville and later Dunnsville, after two pioneer families. Finally, Judge James Tracy Morehead (at right) settled the matter by suggesting the name "Grape Vine" because of the wild mustang grapes so abundant in the area and the proximity to the springs and prairie of the same name. The "Grape Vine" postal cover (above), dated December 5, 1860, is owned by Pamela L. Price. On January 12, 1914, the U.S. Postal Service changed the name to "Grapevine."

Raising cattle was the major enterprise prior to the Civil War, because the soil was difficult to till until better plows were developed. By 1877, modern plows were in use on the black soils of Grape Vine Prairie and, with the invention of barbed wire, open range livestock operations came to an end. Cotton, grain, corn, truck crops, and dairy products all brought modest prosperity. Farmers (above) loaded wheat on their mule-drawn wagons. Below, father and children display their load of hay after a long day's work. The entire family worked together to build their lives on the Grape Vine Prairie, where life was difficult and the challenges seemed insurmountable. But through hard work and perseverance, the families bound together to make a community called Grape Vine.

After the invention of the steel plow, farming became the primary occupation throughout the South, and cotton was the major cash crop. In the fall, the fields around Grapevine were white with cotton and ready for harvest. Around 1930, Claude Parker worked in a cotton field south of town, pulling cotton bolls and putting them in a canvas cotton sack that could hold as much as 100 pounds.

In order to share this part of Grapevine's agricultural past, cotton is grown in a small plot at Nash Farm, the oldest intact farmstead in Tarrant County, located near downtown Grapevine. Visitors, young and old, have the opportunity to see cotton growing, feel the prickly cotton bolls, and imagine what it would be like to work all day in the Texas heat "pickin' cotton."

After the cotton was picked, it was loaded onto wagons and taken to a cotton gin. The influx of new residents, both African American and white, from the South after the Civil War created an experienced labor force. This photograph taken in the early 1900s shows the cotton gin at West College and Scribner Streets. Henry H. Yancy, in the center foreground, was manager.

This cotton gin had piles of cotton burrs left after the ginning process was completed. The gin separated the cotton fiber from the seeds and burrs. After the invention of the gin, one man could do the work once done by 50 men picking out seeds by hand. The farmers in Grapevine were fortunate to have several gins to use during cotton season.

Opened around 1875 and located at Scribner and Wall Streets, the Farmers Gin is shown with five workers surrounded by bales of cotton, each weighing as much as 500 pounds. In the 1930s, Jesse Horn Wright worked as the ginner during cotton time and later bought and renamed it the Wright Gin Company. Since ginning is seasonal, Wright opened the Basket Factory near the gin in 1938, giving employment in the off-season to local citizens.

In the 1920s through the late 1940s, dairy farms were extremely important to the economy of the rural areas around Grapevine. Cows and the farmers, like George Hurst (above), who milked those cows by hand twice a day, were a familiar sight. Ed Havran, another local dairyman, collected historical information, founded the Texas Dairy Heritage Foundation, and donated a major exhibit of artifacts to the Grapevine Historical Museum.

Cotton was not the only crop on the Grape Vine Prairie; wisely, the farmers diversified. This was possible because the area offered a dependable water supply and rich soil, welcoming the farmer who set down roots. In 1921, Edward Thomas Simmons's steam engine and thrashing machine are shown at work on his farm, which is now part of the Dallas-Fort Worth International Airport.

In the 1920s, Emmett Forbes was one of the first to raise watermelons, cantaloupes, and tomatoes for the markets in Fort Worth and Dallas. At gathering time, entire families were hired to pick and cull the crops, which were sold at the farmers markets. This load of 24 watermelons, weighing an average of 56 pounds, was headed to the Dallas Market.

In the 1940s, Leonard Hall, born and reared in Grapevine, grew cantaloupes. He is pictured holding some of his prized melons in his cantaloupe field before they are taken to market. Today this same farmland is used to grow grapes at the Delaney Vineyard beside State Highway 121 (below). Grapevine invited the Texas Wine and Grape Growers Association to move its headquarters to Grapevine in the 1990s and extended the invitation to Texas wineries to establish vineyards and open tasting rooms. This venture has proved very successful and celebrates Grapevine's agricultural past through this new industry.

The Grapevine Cannery workers are pictured here in 1936 with Mayor Benjamin Richard Wall (center holding his cane), who facilitated the cannery's opening in Grapevine. This proved to be a tremendous help in providing food and employment during the Great Depression, as well as giving all a place to can their own produce from their gardens.

Earl Copeland built the Grapevine Ice Company in 1940. During the summers, ice was a welcome relief to the Texas heat. The company delivered ice to Grapevine and surrounding towns. Each home had an "ice card" to place in the window to indicate the size of the block of ice the family wished to purchase and place in their "ice box." Operation of the plant was discontinued in the early 1970s. The scale used for weighing the ice is on display in the Grapevine Historical Museum.

20

Jesse James Hall, born in 1904, was the first farmer in the Grapevine area to buy a tractor. Many vegetables were grown on his farm, but tomatoes and cantaloupe were his specialties, and the annual Cantaloupe Festival was a very important event for him. Hall (right) examined tomatoes before taking them to market. In the photograph below, his large truck is loaded with produce as he takes time to pose with his children in the early 1940s. Years earlier, as a child, Hall had helped his father haul vegetables to market in Dallas by horse-drawn wagon on unpaved roads. His farm and home are located in Grapevine on the street that bears his name, Hall-Johnson Road.

As the rails were laid in the late 1880s (above), the citizens looked with great expectations to the future of their farming community. The Cotton Belt Railroad, completed in 1888, was key to the progress and prosperity of Grape Vine. Captured in this 1925 photograph (below) are two gentlemen waiting for the train, with the mailbag nearby ready for pickup.

A group of Grape Vine citizens stands ready to go by train to Fort Worth for a political rally in 1908. Among them, instruments in hand, are the members of the Grape Vine Cornet Band. Joseph Weldon Bailey was running for office and became a U.S. senator from Texas. He has been called "one of the last of the State's old-timed silver-tongued orators and fiery political campaigners."

Today the Grapevine Vintage Railroad travels along the historic Cotton Belt Route between Grapevine and the Fort Worth Stockyards. The train is pulled by the 1896 steam engine (above), which is the oldest continuously operating steam engine in the south, as well as a vintage diesel locomotive from 1953. The train has authentic 1920s and 1930s Victorian-style coaches, re-creating for its 21st-century passengers the experience as it was in the glory days of rail travel.

Hugh Corbin took Myrt Wall riding in his "courting cart" pulled by his "stepping horse," Mabel. About the time this picture was taken in 1908, Corbin was the only student in the first graduating class of Grape Vine public schools.

Nash Groover, grandson of Thomas Jefferson Nash, bought the first automobile in Grape Vine. He and his car were nearly banned from the Grape Vine streets by its citizens, because the noise caused such a commotion with the horses. Runaway buggies and wagons made for unhappy neighbors.

24

GRAPEVINE PRODUCING CO.

The citizens of Grapevine, and others from the surrounding area, gathered in 1919 with excitement and anticipation for what could have been a landmark oil discovery. The Grapevine Producing Company sold $10 shares for the purpose of drilling for oil and gas on a lease of 10,000 acres just west of Grapevine. The company scheduled the time when they were to strike oil, and the people, dressed in their Sunday best, gathered for the big event and posed for this picture, which can be seen in the Grapevine Historical Museum. Unfortunately, it was a dry hole, and everyone left greatly disappointed. Ninety years later, drilling for natural gas has become a priority again, leading to active gas wells all around Grapevine today. Many citizens and establishments have enjoyed sizable profits.

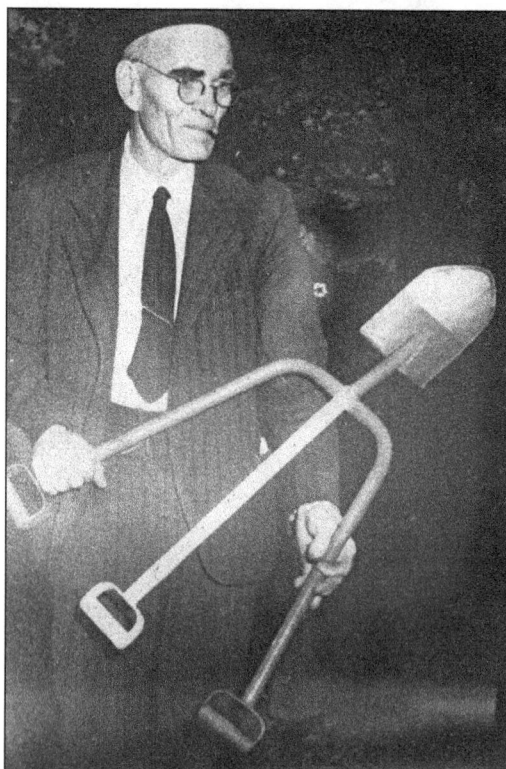

In 1948, officials broke ground to begin construction on the Grapevine Dam and Reservoir project, which was completed in 1952. The U.S. Army Corps of Engineers started this project to impound the watershed of Denton Creek for flood control, recreation, and a water supply for Grapevine and three Dallas County municipalities, including Dallas. The three-handled shovel was designed and made especially for the occasion by local blacksmith Charlie Millican (at left). The three handles represented the U.S. government, the City of Grapevine, and the City of Dallas. The shovel is kept at the Grapevine Historical Museum.

In 1951, workmen had almost completed the Grapevine Dam, located about 1 mile northeast of town. Lake Grapevine has become a great asset to the community as well as to the North Texas area for its flood control and water conservation and for being a key recreational center. The federal government purchased more than 17,900 acres of land for its construction, causing many citizens to relocate their farms and homes and find other livelihoods.

Workmen parked on the spillway during construction of the Grapevine Dam in the early 1950s. The U.S. Army Corps of Engineers predicted it would take five years to fill the lake. However, the lake filled before all of Jinks Benjamin Jones's equipment could be moved. He had farmed until the new lake began to infringe on much of his land. His equipment remains on the bottom of Lake Grapevine, providing a breeding ground for fish.

In 1957, the North Texas area experienced heavy rains, and the lake filled up so rapidly that, even with the floodgates open, water came over the spillway and damaged the road east of it. Citizens went to see this overflow, and using an early surfing technique, children slid down the spillway on pieces of cardboard.

A two-lane paved road was built across the top of Grapevine Dam, which is 28 feet thick, 12,850 feet wide, and 137 feet tall. This car, in the mid-1950s, parked at the access to the Lake Grapevine gate tower. In the background is the lake, which has 7,280 acres of water and 60 miles of shoreline at conservation level.

Dinosaur tracks were uncovered by flooding in 1981 when water from the spillway washed away the road below the Grapevine Dam. Since that time, when the lake levels drop, additional tracks have been located. The U.S. Army Corps of Engineers believes these are the footprints of a Hadrosaur, a duck-billed dinosaur. Two young visitors, Harrison and Hudson, are shown above with a cast replica of these footprints in the Grapevine Historical Museum. Pictured below is the Plesiosaur, unearthed in 1972 south of Grapevine during preliminary excavation for the Dallas-Fort Worth Regional Airport. The remains of this 25-foot-long prehistoric creature are dated at being 70 million years old.

In 1918, World War I pilots from the Royal Flying Corps and U.S. Army Air Forces trained at Camp Taliaferrio in Fort Worth. They would practice landing and taking off in a pasture east of Grapevine's downtown area. One can imagine the excitement this caused. Mary Virginia Wall Simmons, a young girl at the time, remembered that the boys wanted to climb out the school window to take a closer look.

When the Dallas-Fort Worth Regional Airport opened on January 13, 1974, two-thirds of it was located within the city limits of Grapevine. This has greatly impacted the community in a positive way. In contrast to the occasional plane landing in a pasture in 1918, some 3,000 airplanes landed and took off daily in 2009 at the international airport, bringing millions of visitors to this historic Texas prairie community.

This aerial photograph of Dallas-Fort Worth Regional Airport, taken around 1977, looks northward. Grapevine is shown in the upper left corner, and Lake Grapevine is at the top. Built on prime farmland, the airport displaced about 700 people, including many who were direct descendants of settlers who came to the Grape Vine Prairie in the 1840s and 1850s. A few of the farmers, who sold their land north of town when Lake Grapevine was built, had purchased farms on the south side of town. They again had to relocate, this time for the new airport.

Above, the first landing of a supersonic Concorde in the United States occurred at Dallas-Fort Worth Regional Airport in the fall of 1973 to commemorate the airport's completion. The Concorde had arrived from England. On January 12, 1979, two Concorde jets (below) flew from the East Coast and lined up to land on parallel runways at Dallas-Fort Worth Regional Airport. It was acclaimed as a great day in air travel, and this began supersonic service out of the airport.

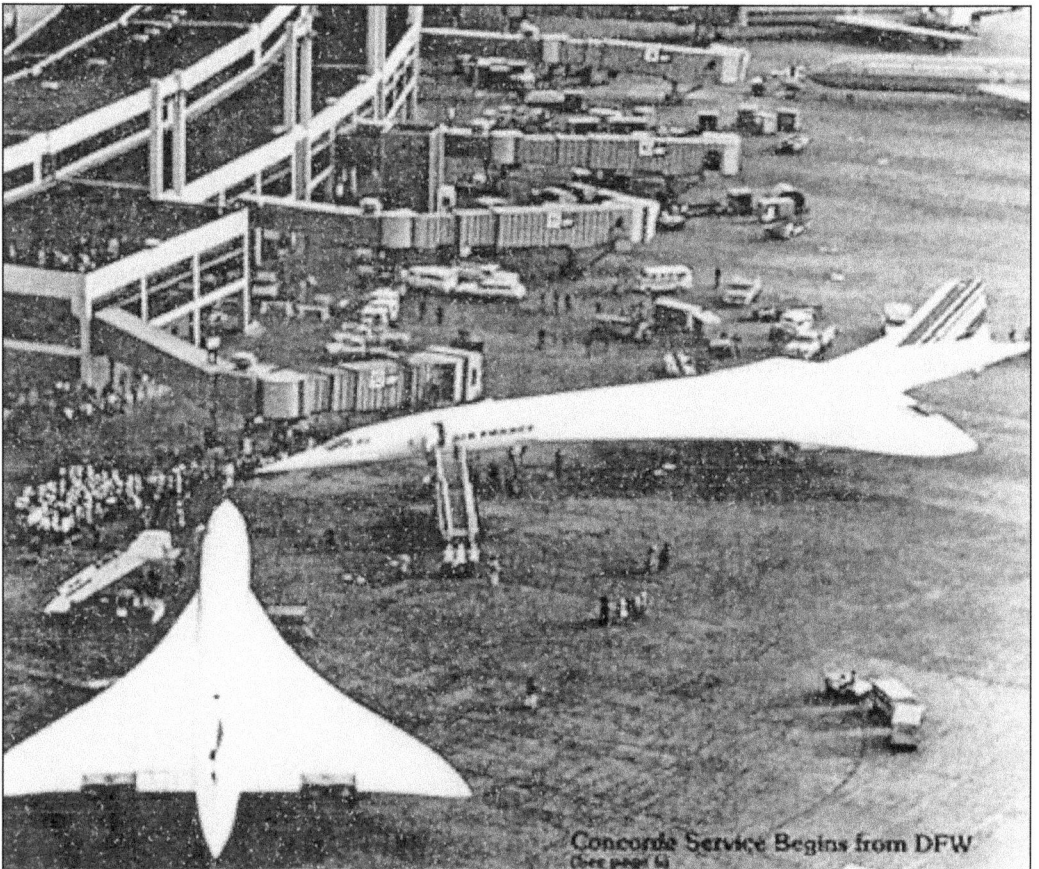

Concorde Service Begins from DFW
(See page 6)

The original name of the airport was Dallas-Fort Worth Regional Airport until 1985, when the name was changed to the Dallas-Fort Worth International Airport. The control tower near the center of the airport directs all arriving and departing flights. The airport is larger than the island of Manhattan in New York with 18,076 acres. In land area, it is the largest airport in Texas and the second largest in the United States.

In 2005, the Dallas-Fort Worth International Airport expanded by adding the international Terminal D, more runways, and the Grand Hyatt Hotel. It is the ninth-busiest international gateway in the United States and is the largest and main hub for American Airlines. In 2008, around 57 million passengers passed through the airport and about 19 million of those visited Grapevine. It has truly helped Grapevine become a door to the world, with thousands of international visitors stopping by to see a Texas prairie town.

The Founders Plaza, which overlooks the northwest quadrant of the Dallas-Fort Worth International Airport, is a tribute to airport founders. The site features one of Grapevine's sculptures, entitled *Share the Dream* by artist Dennis Smith. The plaza also has a place to observe some of the 3,000 airplanes that land and take off daily and is equipped with audio to hear tower communications.

Terminal D at Dallas-Fort Worth International Airport is the official port of entry for all returning military personnel. Because the airport is less than five minutes from downtown Grapevine, citizens and visitors, both young and old, meet these planes of returning servicemen and give these American heroes and their families a warm Texas welcome.

Two

DOWNTOWN
WHERE EVERYTHING IS WAITING

The citizens of Grapevine have always found reasons to go downtown. Here in 1899, people gather for the Binder Parade down Main Street. The new farm equipment available for use on the Grape Vine Prairie was paraded down Main Street for farmers to view. This photograph was taken looking northwest from the corner of Main and Worth Streets and shows many of the established businesses and buildings, some of which are still standing.

What is considered to be one of the oldest standing brick buildings on Main Street was constructed about 1889. Originally it housed a general store that also sold funeral supplies and was owned and operated by the John Edward Foust family. In 1945, the funeral business was moved south on Main Street.

Clifford Jenkins Wall, on the right, owned and operated the Wall Drug Store founded by his father, Zachary Taylor Wall, in 1872. It was located in a building constructed in 1900 at 320 South Main Street. In 1918, "Cliff" Wall sold the drugstore to John A. Spinks, who later sold it to Roy Chambers. In the late 1940s, Chambers moved the business to 406 South Main Street, changing the name to City Drug.

In 1903, members of the Grape Vine Cornet Band built a bandstand near the corner of Main and Texas Streets for their performances. This smartly uniformed band was honored in 1904 to play in Fort Worth when Pres. Teddy Roosevelt visited Texas. John Randolph Willingham, the bandmaster, is in his business suit on the steps, and his daughter Linnie Willingham, who later married George L. Bushong, is standing in the front.

Looking southwest down Main Street around 1900, the storefront architecture was typical of this era. Horse-drawn carriages and wagons traveled down a dusty Main Street bordered by a plank sidewalk that served as a gathering place for local townspeople coming in to shop. The name, "Drug Store," on the building advertised its occupant's business, and the utility poles proudly displayed the signs of progress.

Taken about 1910, this photograph looks north on Main Street. The population of Grapevine was 700 and there were a few cars, though buggies and wagons were still the main transportation. The Wood-Wall Realty Company, the livery stable, and the bandstand are pictured on the east side of the street. In the background, houses formed a frame around Main Street.

Benjamin Richard Wall (on the porch) watches as Edward Thomas Simmons (front left), John Benjamin Wood (right), and another unidentified friend show their horses in front of the Wood-Wall Realty Company, which was opened in 1907.

Looking northeast on Main Street, Barton Harry Starr Jr. and his father-in-law, Sandy Alexander Wall, can be seen standing in the door of their livery stable. They operated this business, located where the Gazebo now stands, until automobiles took the place of horses. The two were also partners in the dray business, unloading and delivering merchandise that came to Grapevine by railroad.

Charles Marion Millican began his career as a blacksmith on a farm and came to town in 1908 to work for another man. He started his own shop in 1909 and worked there for 50 years with his son Bill Charles Millican. His building was at Main and Texas Streets and, in 1929, he rebuilt the same structure a few feet south so Texas Street could be extended through his site.

The feed store, owned by William Douglas Deacon, faced South Main Street in the area where the Gazebo is now located. His wife, Edna Maude Deacon, had prepared a successful mixture of chicken feed at her farm and later moved her hatchery to a location behind the feed store. In 1936, B&D Mills was established and later a hatchery was built across from the mill.

In 1916, Frank Estill, a local builder and a Tarrant County commissioner, constructed an automobile sales and service building for John B. Wood, and in 1920, county road workers gathered there before work. In this same building, in 1937, James "Jim" Newton Wood opened a Western Auto Store. His first customer was his nine-year-old son Charles William Wood, who later operated the business until he retired in 1991 after having a "closing business" sale.

Looking northwest down Main Street, this photograph taken around 1912 shows the town bustling with activity. The Lucas Building (left) was followed by the Morrow Building, where the drugstore and the Grapevine Home Bank were located. Farther north were the Yates Building and another bank. Across the street, men gathered to look at a new automobile.

In 1914, William R. Buckner established a grocery business in Grapevine and used this wagon to deliver groceries in the local area. His son Jerome Kirby Buckner joined the business following World War I. Kirby moved the grocery business in 1930 to 308 South Main. In the late 1930s, he added a dry goods and hardware department and introduced the city to serve-yourself shopping carts.

The Grapevine Telephone Company Exchange and Dr. O. O. Hollingsworth's dental office were located upstairs in this building. Downstairs were the Mabry Drugstore and the *Grapevine Sun*, founded by Benjamin Richard Wall in November 1895. Wall sold the paper after two years to J. E. Keeling. Keeling's son William Edward (below) started helping him with the newspaper in 1903 at the age of 14. Under this father-son union, the newspaper became a leader among North Texas weeklies, being noted especially for consistent typographical excellence, factual reporting, and wholesome news items concerning community activities. The business was passed down to a third-generation family member Zena Keeling Oxford and her husband, Gene Oxford. It stayed under the Keeling management for 79 years. The *Grapevine Sun* closed April 30, 2009, after 114 years of serving the Grapevine community.

Telephone operators Maude Livingston (center) and Launa France (right) work as telephone operators at the switchboard for the Grapevine Telephone Company housed on the second floor of the Odd Fellows building. Nora Bell McPherson Livingston (left) checks telephone records. As operators in a small town, they always knew their customers.

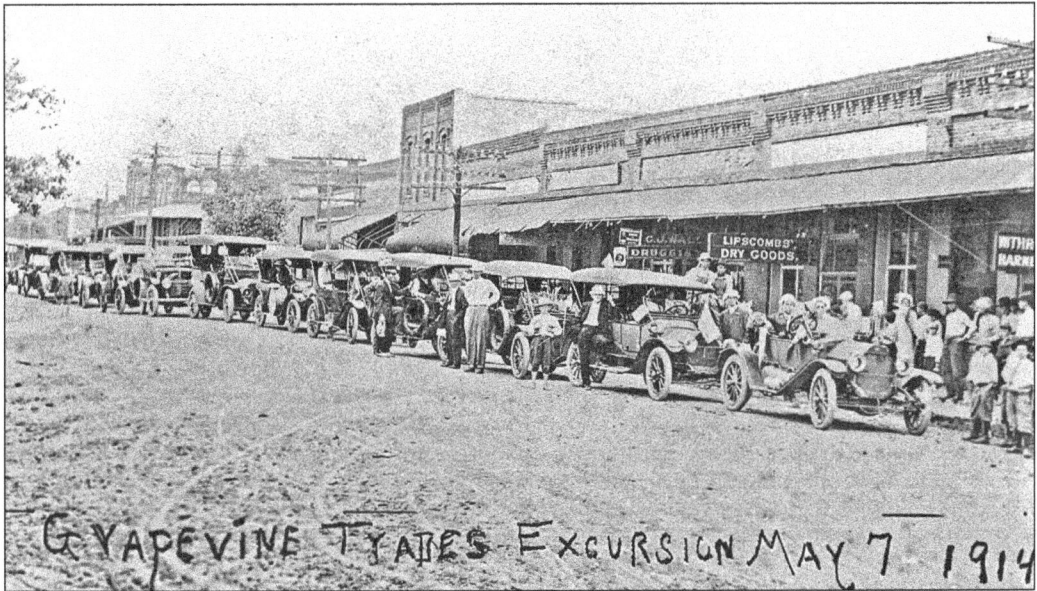

A parade of automobiles, an "excursion," was organized and headed north on Main Street on May 7, 1914, to travel to other communities to promote Grapevine. Signs advertising C. J. Wall Drugstore, Lipscomb Dry Goods, and Withrow Harness Shop can be seen above each door. Today all of these buildings have been renovated and are occupied by other businesses.

In 1921, Andrew Wiley "A. W." Willhoite and Bart Starr Jr. opened the first one-stop automobile service in this converted two-story retail building, pictured above. Willhoite's son Wiley Deloys "Ted" Willhoite installed the town's first electric gas pumps and hydraulic auto-lift. The service station closed in 1976 after 55 years of operation by the Willhoites. The picture below, taken around 1932, shows the location on Main Street as well as the correct spelling of the Willhoite Garage and a sign advertising a restroom for ladies. Also visible on the same side of the street are the drugstore and the Lucas Building, which housed a grocery, furniture, and farm implements store on its first floor and funeral supplies on the second story. This store was owned by Joseph Thomas Lucas and passed down through the family.

The U.S. post office in Grapevine was located on the west side of Main Street. Standing in front of the post office around 1923 are, from left to right, postmaster McKinley H. "Max" Frank; his wife, Starr Walker Frank, known as Grapevine's "Grand Lady of Music" because of her talent as a pianist; Juanita Henderson; George E. Hurst; Henry "Bud" Saunders; Will Bennett; and Jim Hamilton.

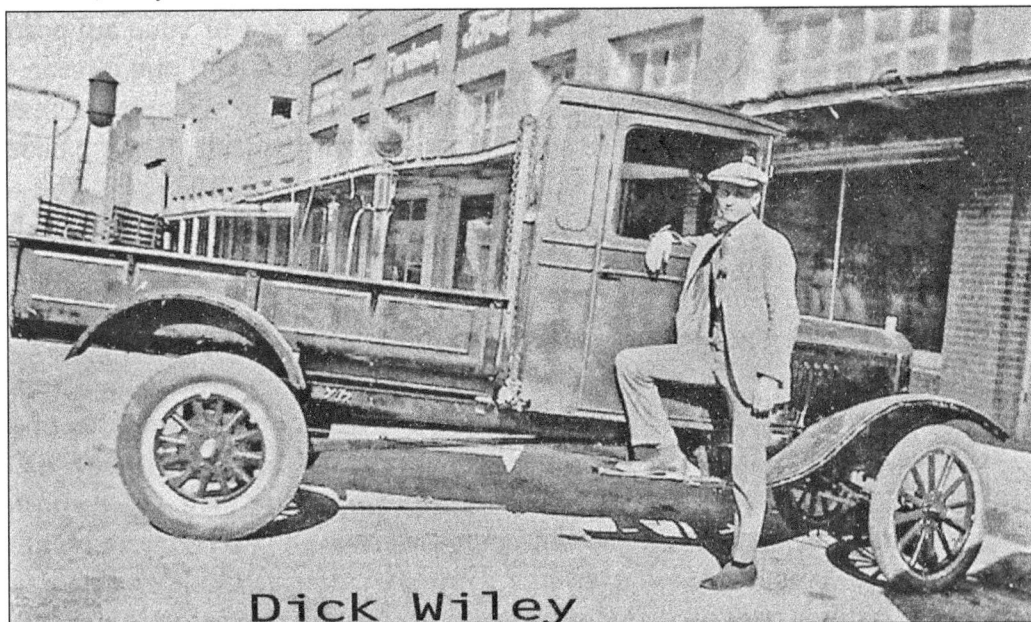

Dick Wiley posed in front of the Ford Dealership on Main Street in 1923. He was hired by local merchants to promote shopping in Grapevine and worked as a salesman and mechanic at the Grapevine Motor Company.

In 1911, Jack Robinson constructed these three buildings on the east side of Grapevine's Main Street for his mercantile business. The south end was originally a two-story structure, and the second floor was home to the Woodmen of the World, which had the largest meeting hall in Grapevine. The water tower was erected in 1925 and remained on the east side of Main Street until a new one was constructed in 1954 on the west side at Barton and Texas Streets.

This view of the 300 block of Main Street around 1925 looks north and shows a paved street with parking in the center of the road. The farming village bustles with activity, as farmers sell their produce, neighbors socialize, and vehicles line the street. Visible on the left are the columns at the front of the Farmers National Bank. These buildings and others to the north have been restored and are in use today.

In the 1920s, with Robert E. "Bob" Morrow (left), the owner and operator of the Grapevine Home Bank, are Henry Clinton Yancey, a bank cashier and owner of Yancey Insurance Agency, and D. E. Throop. Morrow closed the bank in 1933 because of the moratorium initiated by President Roosevelt. He said, "No one is going to tell me how to run my bank."

A group of citizens gathered in front of the Grapevine Home Bank the morning after members of Bonnie and Clyde's gang, J. Les "Red" Stewart and Odell Chambless, robbed it in 1932. Bonnie Parker and Clyde Barrow later killed two state highway patrolmen near Grapevine on State Highway 114 and Dove Road.

47

In 1909, the Grape Vine City Council authorized the building of the Grape Vine Calaboose, located at the southwest corner of Texas and Barton Streets, as its first jail. This structure is a reminder of the seriousness of pioneer justice that lingered into the 20th century. The barrel-vaulted structure is made of 8-inch thick reinforced concrete and has an iron grate door and two small windows. It was moved and restored at the corner of Franklin and Main Streets in 1994.

Built in 1929, the Gulf station at 530 South Main Street was owned by Oscar Thomas and run by Freddie Forrest "Abie" Statum (right) with a coworker known as "Wimpie." Abie's Service Station was dubbed "The Grapevine Men's and Boys' Sports Club," because the guys gathered there in the 1940s, 1950s, and 1960s to play checkers and share hunting, fishing, and sports stories as well as an occasional joke or two.

The Yates House was built at 523 South Main Street sometime around 1870 and was given to Junius Edward Merritt "June" Yates and his bride, Kate Jenkins, by her parents around 1876. The home remained in the Yates family until it was sold in 1941 to John Edward Foust II and his wife, Lillie, owners of J. E. Foust and Sons Funeral Home. Since then, the house has had major alterations and additions. The funeral home celebrated its 100th anniversary in 1980 by placing a time vault on the south lawn to be opened in 2080. Also at that time, the original carriage house was moved to the north side of the funeral home to display the old hearse purchased in 1904 by J. E. Foust I. Three generations of Fousts have carried on the legacy of the family-operated funeral home.

In 1933, Kirby Buckner and W. D. "Bill" Deacon bought a flour mill that was constructed in 1902 at 213 West Hudgins Street and converted it into a feed manufacturing complex. Deacon and sons, Floyd and Earl, ran the business together until 1975. It evolved from a small business to a multistate operation, and the mill was the largest employer in Grapevine for many years.

An aerial view of downtown Grapevine, looking north down Main Street, was taken around 1940. The population was 1,043, and the city's growth appeared to be headed east. Businesses had begun to develop along Northwest Highway, a major east-west thoroughfare opened in 1932.

50

Three

PRESERVATION
APPRECIATING THE PAST

A *Wilderness Welcome* by the city's resident sculptor Archie St. Clair commemorates the pioneers' first view and settlement of the Texas prairie. This life-sized ensemble of wildlife includes deer, bear, a snake, and, of course, grapevines, for which the town is named. Located at the intersection of Main Street and Northwest Highway, it is one of several public art displays in historic downtown Grapevine, where honoring and preserving the past has enhanced the present and guides the future.

Benjamin Richard "B. R." Wall is pictured in the front left with his brother Clifford Jenkins Wall (center, back) and their first cousins. B. R. was born in Grape Vine in 1876, attended the Grape Vine Free School, Grape Vine College, and later, Baylor University, where he studied law. In 1915, he passed the state bar exam with one of the highest scores. The State Bar of Texas issued him Card No. 1, which he carried all his life. B. R. became mayor of Grapevine in 1912 and served 20 years over intermittent terms until 1946. He was mayor during World Wars I and II, and his weekly newspaper columns in the *Grapevine Sun* kept the citizens motivated and optimistic about their future. The bronze sculpture by Archie St. Clair (below) is near the city hall at Main and Wall Streets and honors this great man for his many services to his beloved community.

Grapevine, Texas

Radio _____ Confirm CW SSB QSO of _____ 19 _____

at _____ G.M.T. Ur sigs RST _____ Band _____ MC. _____

W5OLG

XMTR: 32S3 – BTI LK 2000 TH 6 Beam   Rcvr: 75S3B

P. O. Box 261, Tarrant County, Grapevine, Texas, 76051.

Please QSL. Tnx   73 Bob

PITCAIRN ISLAND

VR6TC

Op: Tom Christian

QSO WITH	DATE	GMT	MHZ	RST	2 WAY

HALLICRAFTERS EQUIPMENT   THIS QSO VERIFIED BY W5OLG
HY-GAIN BEAM ANTENNA
ELECTRO-VOICE MIKE
ALL WORKING VY FB   _____

Ham Radio Call Letters

A true civic leader, Benjamin Richard Wall was extremely benevolent and altruistic. These attributes led him to initiate an international relationship with the citizens of Pitcairn, deemed the loneliest island in the Pacific, where most of the inhabitants were descendants of the HMS *Bounty* mutineers. Hearing of the destitute condition of the citizens there, Wall sent magazines and newspapers to islander Lincoln Clark, a shipwrecked American seaman. Thus began a friendship through the mail that continued for over 50 years. Mayor Wall challenged Grapevine citizens to place items for Pitcairn Islanders in a box kept in his office. When the box became full, the shipment was made. Later Robert Stark, Grapevine citizen and ham radio operator, using the above call letters, had frequent contact with Tom Christian. Christian was a descendant of Fletcher Christian, the leader of the mutiny on the HMS *Bounty*, whose story was the inspiration for the books and movies, *Mutiny on the Bounty*. The radio log and transmitter are on display in the Grapevine Historical Museum.

The building at 413 South Main Street burned down in 1938 and was rebuilt in the 1940s. Once completed, the structure was used as the Grapevine City Hall with offices for the library and fire department. The new Grapevine City Hall (below), erected in 1997, is designed to reflect the architectural traditions of Grapevine in the late 19th century. Using historic photographs of buildings now gone, architects created unique architectural elements for the new redbrick structure. The stone pediment, columns, and facade on Main Street are replications of the old Grapevine Farmers National Bank. Atop the new city hall is the bronze sculpture of the *Grapevine Nightwatchman* keeping vigil over the town with his lantern. The statue honors the men who patrolled and protected citizens from 1907 to 1956.

Liberty Park Plaza on Main Street is home to several important aspects of Main Street life. This area was the site where the first government in Grapevine was organized in 1854 by pioneers who planned the city, created its name, and decided on some of the beginning rules of city government. Grapevine was incorporated on February 12, 1907. Standing as a sentinel to the past is the windmill, symbolic of the 29 windmills in Grapevine in the early 1900s. Behind it is the Torian Cabin, built of hand-hewn logs around 1845 by Francis Throop, a Peters Colonist. Later it was sold to John Torian, whose family occupied it until the 1940s. It was moved to this location in 1976 through the efforts of the Grapevine Historical Society and the Grapevine Convention and Visitors Bureau.

The Wallis Hotel, built in 1891 at Main and Hudgins Streets, served travelers and salesmen arriving on the train until it was torn down in 1931. Fondly remembered as "The Brick Hotel," it was erected by Johnnie Wallis for his sister Susan Terrill. In 1991, one hundred years after the hotel was opened, the Grapevine Convention and Visitors Bureau broke ground for their new office structure (below), a faithful reconstruction of the Wallis Hotel. Some of the original hotel furniture is showcased in the building, which is also home to the Grapevine Heritage Foundation. *The Sidewalk Judge*, sitting in front of the new building, is a lifelike tribute to an elder generation of men who would sit for hours at the center of town giving unsolicited advice to passersby. Dedicated in 1997, the judge always has a listening ear.

Cleo Tillery's Sno-Cone stand (above) was located at the corner of Main and Texas Streets next door to the Palace Theatre. Shown in this 1950s parade picture, it was a favorite place from 1950 to 2000 for young and old during the warm days of summer. The same location is pictured below in 2010. The Cleo Tillery Bench commemorates this memory of those who lived in the slower-paced community and serves as a welcome invitation to "sit a spell." In 1991, the Grapevine Heritage Foundation, committed to the preservation of Grapevine's history, acquired the Palace Theatre and the Burrus Super Market and completed restoration in 2000. They have been transformed, and the old store, now the Lancaster Theatre, provides a unique performance and meeting facility. The Palace Theatre hosts many events and still shows movies as it did when it was the place to be on a Saturday night.

The citizens and local merchants came together in 1986 and built a beautiful white gazebo as a gift for future generations and in celebration of Texas's sesquicentennial. The Gazebo, a charming replica of 1900s architecture and reminiscent of the first Grapevine Cornet Bandstand, is the center point of life on Grapevine's downtown historic Main Street. It is decorated appropriately throughout the year for each holiday.

The Grapevine Masonic Lodge No. 288 A. F. and A. M., chartered in 1866, purchased the land at 401 South Main Street in 1888 and constructed a small brick building, which was razed in 1916. Erected on the same location, this two-story Masonic building features a meeting hall upstairs for both the Masonic Lodge and the Order of the Eastern Star. The ground floor has always been used for retail space. The mural on the north wall, painted by Jorge D'Soria in 2009, honors famous men who were members of the Masonic Lodge, including George Washington, John Wayne, and astronaut Edwin Eugene "Buzz" Aldrin Jr.

Grapevine is a community that values public art. *The Sunday Skaters* sculpture at 601 South Main Street, created by Archie St. Clair, is a collection of life-sized figures that represent the 1920s and 1930s. Three happy-go-lucky skaters were created using photographs of the actual Grapevine children of the period, Mary Virginia Wall Simmons, John Edward "Junior" Foust III, and Dorothy Beth Maxwell Francisco, all of whom grew up to be leading Grapevine citizens. Even Muttin, the dog, was patterned after one who belonged to Uncle Jim Daniel, one of the Grapevine Nightwatchmen. *The Homecoming* (below), a two-piece sculpture created by Michael Pavlovsky, is located in front of the Cotton Belt Railroad Depot on South Main Street. The statue depicts a soldier returning from service to a loving embrace. The couples' shoes are somewhat larger, representing that the couple had "big shoes to fill." Each element, from the faceless watch to the ordinal directions at the statue's base, has special meaning.

In 1992, the Grapevine Heritage Foundation relocated the 1901 Grapevine Cotton Belt Railroad Depot to its location along the railroad tracks at 705 South Main Street. The restored depot serves as a ticket office for the train, the visitor information center, and the Grapevine Historical Museum. The museum, which focuses on area history, is owned and operated by the Grapevine Historical Society. Other landmarks are located near the old railroad station, such as the restored 1888 Section Foreman's House (below), where the foreman and his family lived.

In 1995, the Grapevine Blacksmith Shop opened at the Grapevine Heritage Center. It is a replica of Charlie Millican's shop, which was located at Main and Texas Streets. Also found at the Heritage Center are the Bragg House, Vetro Glassblowing Studio, and Archie St. Clair's bronze sculpture studio.

The fallout shelter pictured is typical of those built in the 1950s during the Cold War era. This one was possibly constructed after the Jack Patterson family purchased property in the 1600 block of West Wall Street from the A. C. Corbin family in 1954. Paul W. McCallum, executive director of the Grapevine Convention and Visitors Bureau, saved it and moved it to the Grapevine Heritage Center. Today it is considered a curiosity.

Interlocking Tower 16 was built in 1903 and moved in 2002 from Sherman to Grapevine and has since been restored. It served as a lookout post to control the flow of train traffic and to mechanically switch trains from one track to another. Men used the old tower's levers, dials, and toggle switches to regulate the movements of the trains. Computers do this job today.

The turntable for the Grapevine Vintage Railroad was purchased in 1992 for $1 from the Santa Fe Railroad in Saginaw. The price was right, but moving it to its present location was a major production requiring heavy-duty oil field equipment and cranes. Grapevine needed a turntable in order to operate the Grapevine Vintage Railroad and to turn its vintage steam engine, *Puffy*, around.

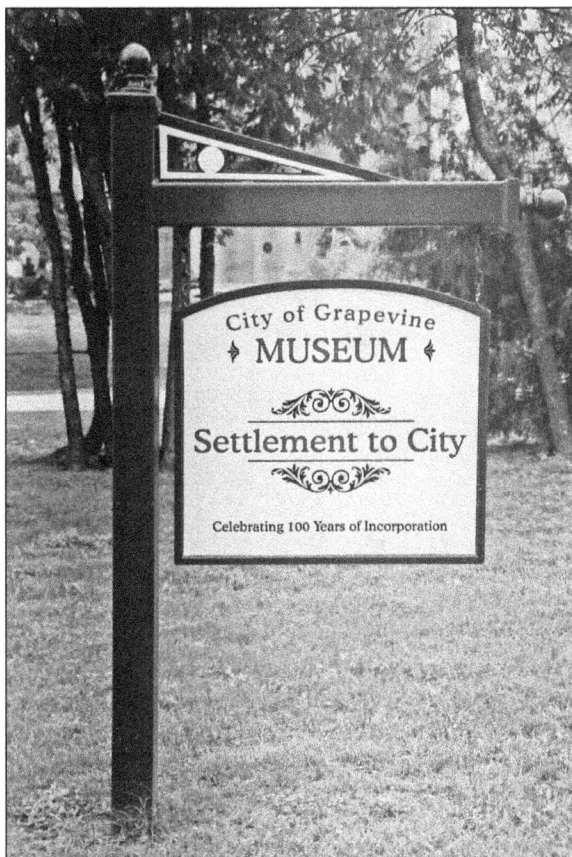

On February 12, 1907, citizens of Grape Vine voted to incorporate the town as a municipal government and to provide services for the growing settlement. In 2007, Grapevine marked the centennial of incorporation by debuting the Settlement to City Museum in the Keeling House. The museum officially opened at GrapeFest 2009 and features a time line, photographs, and artifacts, which tell the story of the city's development. Rev. E. Nathan Hudgins, founder of what is today known as First United Methodist Church Grapevine, built the house below around 1888. James E. Keeling, owner of the *Grapevine Sun*, later owned it.

The house built in 1869 by Elizabeth (née Nasher) and Thomas J. Nash is located on Tarrant County's oldest intact farmstead. When the couple came to Grapevine from Kentucky in 1859, they and their children lived in a log house near the present structure. This picture was probably taken soon after Thomas J. Nash died in 1906.

In 1950, the Nash Farmhouse stood surrounded by 110 acres of rich farmland. Visible from this aerial view are the main house, a henhouse, and the large barn.

64

Restored to its original grandeur in 2008, the Nash Farmhouse and barn at 626 Ball Street stand as a testimony to the Grapevine Heritage Foundation's focus to keep history alive in Grapevine. "The farm's story and the lessons of life that children will learn here will live on and on," stated Melva Stanfield, chairman of the Grapevine Heritage Foundation. Nash Farm is listed on the National Register of Historic Places.

Inez Davis Jewett and her husband, Harlan Jewett, stand on the front porch of the restored Nash Farmhouse in 2008. They are holding a picture of Inez standing in the exact spot on the porch some 80 years earlier. Inez grew up in the Davis House across the road from the Nash Farm and played with the children who lived there.

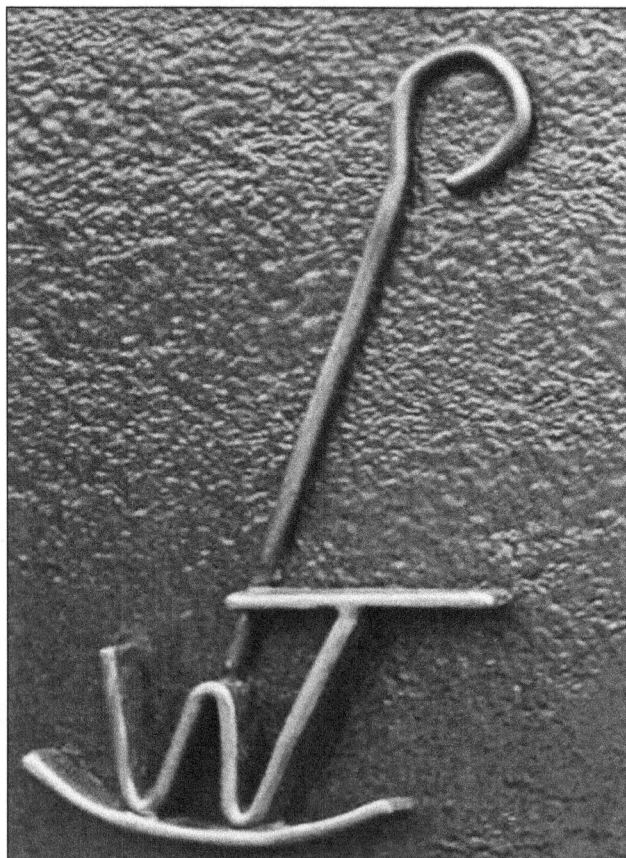

The old barn at Nash Farm is the place to be in the spring when baby animals are being born and the crops are being planted. Volunteers help raise sheep, calves, and goats to show to visitors. On one end of the barn is a marker with Wiley Deloys "Ted" Willhoite's brand, the Rockin' TW, placed there in his memory by the Grapevine Heritage Foundation and the City of Grapevine. Born in 1911, he was a lifelong resident of Grapevine, a devoted Christian who was a member of the First United Methodist Church Grapevine for 82 years, and an avid golfer. The dedication marker reads, "Most of all, Ted was a warm, loving person who served his community with joy and humor and helped make and preserve its history."

Four

HOME
WHERE THE STORY BEGAN

The Torian Cabin, originally located on Dove Road 4 miles northwest of Grapevine, is shown as it appeared around 1886 when John R. Torian, a farmer from Kentucky, bought it for his wife, Dulcie, and their three children. Pictured here are, from left to right, W. T. Sowers, John R. Torian, and his daughter Ella Torian. The cabin was constructed by Francis Throop, a Peters Colonist from Missouri, in about 1845 and was occupied until the 1940s. The cabin, the oldest structure in Tarrant County, was moved in 1976 to historic downtown Grapevine in Liberty Park Plaza at 203 South Main Street.

Located at 213 East College Street and constructed in the popular arts and crafts style in 1926, this brick house belonged to Robert Morrow, the successful and thrifty owner and president of Grapevine Home Bank.

This craftsman-influenced house at 214 East College Street was constructed in 1908 for Grapevine dentist Dr. Orlando O. Hollingsworth and his wife, Ione (née Dorris). He was mayor of Grapevine for one year before resigning to serve on the school board. He was active in civic affairs, particularly on behalf of education, and sang in the First Baptist Church choir. Ione's parents, Dr. Thomas Dorris and Anne Eliza (née Caster), lived next door at 224 East College Street.

Built around 1915 for Anna V. (née Lipscomb) and Clarence Emory Stewart (1860–1946), this two-story brick Prairie School house located at 223 East College Street is one of the more substantial homes in Grapevine. The house was purchased in 1917 by the parents of Clarence Emory "Pie" Stewart (1889–1937)—Mattie E. (née Giddens) and William Robert Stewart (1856–1918), the brother of the former Clarence Emory. The younger Clarence Emory "Pie" owned the Olympia Confectionery, which later became City Drug, and lived in this house until he died.

The Mary Lipscomb Wiggins House (above), constructed around 1905 at 307 East College Street, was designed by Fort Worth architect Frank Singleton. Across the street, the Stewart House (top picture), mirrors the Wiggins House. Mary Wiggins graduated in 1896 from the institute that became Texas Christian University and placed great value on education. A girl's dormitory at her alma mater bears her name.

Dr. Thomas Benton Dorris, one of the early physicians in Grapevine, arrived in 1885 and built this Queen Anne–style home at 224 East College Street in 1896 for his wife, Ann Eliza (née Caster), and daughter, Ione. Dr. Dorris was very active in the community. He taught a Red Cross class of nursing during World War I and was the surgeon for the railroad. He was one of five members of the First Baptist Church Building Committee and the only one to live to see the building completed. His grandson Dr. Borden B. Hollingsworth described his grandfather as "the ideal picture of a kind-hearted, efficient physician and friend, a good citizen, and a sincere Christian" until his death in 1918. Dr. Dorris is shown riding home in his carriage after making a visit southeast of Grapevine about 1912.

The house above, built in 1924 for Frances Lucas (née Pyatt) and Robert Lee Lucas, a local mortician, was typical of the modest bungalows constructed for Grapevine's growing middle class in the 1920s. It is located at 314 East College Street in the historic district.

This brick bungalow, located at 322 East College Street, was constructed in 1934 for Eunice Lipscomb (née Yeates) and Boone Lipscomb, brother of Mary Lipscomb Wiggins. Eunice and Boone loved to host card parties, and their house was built with entertaining in mind. Eunice kept a diary spanning over 55 years. The home, with servants' quarters and a wood barn, was built on the former location of the Grapevine Presbyterian Church.

In 1935, Mattie Mae Wright (née Lucas) and Lemoine Wright built this home at 222 East Franklin Street. Sandstone was popular for exterior finishes in the 1930s. Lemoine owned Wright Lumber Company and later worked with his father at Wright Veneer and Basket Factory until his death in 1945. Mattie Mae was a schoolteacher for many years and lived there until her death in 1984.

This home at 221 East Worth Street, with late Queen Anne Victorian design, was built for Grapevine merchant Wingate Hezekiah Lucas II (1870–1910), who was the father of three sons and a daughter. One of his sons, Wingate III, born in this house, was very influential in the development of Lake Grapevine during his tenure as a U.S. congressman from 1947 to 1954. He and his wife, Jerry (née Clark), had five children in his birthplace and lived in the house until 1954.

Charles and Frank Estill, local builders in the area, constructed this house at 503 East Worth Street in 1908 for Beulah Wall (née Estill) and Clifford Jenkins Wall. Cliff thought "it was so far from Main Street that he bought a bicycle to ride to work" at the drugstore. Their marriage in 1906 joined two Grapevine pioneer families; they had three children: Mary Virginia Wall Simmons, Josephine Wall Wright, and James Estill Wall.

The home at 529 East Worth Street owned by William Edward "Ed" Keeling, who married Grady Wood in 1912, is a late Victorian and arts and crafts style. In 1903, at age 14, Keeling began working with his father, who owned the *Grapevine Sun* and, in 1912, became the publisher of the paper. Ed and Grady worked together at the newspaper.

The Bushong log cabin is the oldest log cabin still occupied in Tarrant County. George Emanuel Bushong, who arrived in 1858 as a well-educated, energetic pioneer, married Elizabeth Ann Jenkins in 1866 and built the cabin in 1871 for their family. He taught school and began to purchase land, much of it at 50¢ per acre. He also built and operated a sawmill, flour mill, and the first cotton gin in this area. They had 13 children, 7 of whom died in infancy. The log cabin has been moved several times, restored, and enlarged and is pictured below as it looks today.

Standing in front of the "Big House," built in 1880 by George Emanuel Bushong, are his grandsons. Shown from left to right are H. T. Burgoon, Charles Brock, George E. Bushong, and Bill Morgan around 1970. Unfortunately this elegant house burned in 1977. In 2003, another "Big House," the Gaylord Texan Resort and Convention Center on Lake Grapevine, was erected on this property.

George Emanuel Bushong built this 1903 Folk-type home located at 212 East Franklin Street for his son George L. Bushong when he married Linnie May Willingham in 1904. Bushong adopted the "L" in his name after he married Linnie. The Bushongs were active in the community and helped organize the original Grapevine Cornet Band. Band rehearsals were frequently held in their home.

David Eckley Box Sr. and Mary Ruth Dougherty were married in 1914. They had this home with indoor plumbing built at Franklin and Dooley Streets in 1921 by her father, John Joseph Dougherty. Box helped to organize the Tarrant County State Bank, which later became First National Bank of Grapevine. He devoted much time to civic activities and helped get State Highway 114 routed through Grapevine.

Wiley Deloys "Ted" Willhoite built this brick house at 528 South Dooley Street in 1944 during World War II. Willhoite had to get special permission from the War Production Board to justify its construction due to shortages of labor and materials. He also used salvaged lumber from the Woodmen of the World Hall. His family lived there three years. When his mother died, they enlarged his father's house at 408 East Worth Street and moved in with him.

Constructed for Lucinda Jo Lipscomb (née Estill) and Edward Jenner Lipscomb around 1907 at 607 South Dooley Street, this Victorian house displays arts and crafts influence. Edward came to Texas from Mississippi after the Civil War and owned and operated the E. J. Lipscomb and Son Dry Goods.

Gertie Hurst (née Corbin) and George Ellison Hurst built their Colonial Revival–style home at 404 East Wall Street about 1909, soon after they were married. George started carrying mail by horseback in the Grapevine area in 1901 and delivered mail for almost 30 years. Their daughter Sue married Joe C. Lipscomb, a surveyor, and lived in this house all but 8 of her 91 years.

Edward Thomas "Ed" Simmons married Martha Elizabeth Withrow in 1898, and they lived from 1915 until 1922 in a farmhouse south of Grapevine that is now a part of Dallas-Fort Worth International Airport. Ed and Martha (above) are shown with four of their five children. In 1923, they moved into a house on Smith Street. In the spring of 1937, their fifth child, James Edward "Hugh" Simmons, built the house (below) in his mother's garden plot for his bride, Mary Virginia Wall.

Earl Yates Sr., who spent most of his life in the dry goods business in Grapevine, had this house (above) built at 405 Smith Street in 1899 for his bride, Kate Estill, by her father, Charles Carmichael Estill. Charles owned a lumberyard and built many houses, but none as special as this one for his eldest daughter. Earl and Kate moved into their home on their wedding night. There they raised six children.

BENJAMIN R. WALL
1876-1955

IDA MAE STULTS WALL
1874-1959

In 1897, after she attended Howard Payne College, Ida Mae Stults (right) married Benjamin Richard Wall, who had spent "a pleasant and profitable year at Baylor," according to granddaughter Nancy Hudson Lewis. Wall was the founder of the *Grapevine Sun*, organizer of the Farmers and Merchants Milling Company, and spent many years in public service to his community. Using plans by the Sanguinet and Staats architectural firm, E. F. Brown built this home at 421 Smith Street in 1904.

THEIR HOME
Corner of Smith and Franklin Streets
Grapevine, Texas   Built 1904

Joseph Priestly Lipscomb, a Confederate veteran, and his bride, Marian Frances Elizabeth Weatherly, moved into this home at 210 West College Street around 1870. This Hall-and-Parlor house has been in the family for 140 years and is one of the oldest homes in Grapevine.

Built around 1918 for Etta Bennett (née Willingham) and William Madison Bennett, Grapevine's first marshal, this bungalow at 218 West College Street has housed five generations. Their daughter Annie Louise Bennett Tate and her husband, Gordon Tate, Grapevine's mayor from 1949 to 1952, also lived there. They were the parents of two children, Sandra and William D., mayor of Grapevine for over 30 years. W. D. Tate's daughter Sheri Tate Thompson, her husband, and their three sons now live in the house.

This craftsman-style home was constructed around 1916 at 215 West College Street for Bonnie Mary Lowe (née Botts) and Ernest E. Lowe, mayor of Grapevine from 1924 to 1932. During his tenure, many major projects were accomplished, including improvements to the city water and sewage systems as well as electricity and telephone services. Construction was also completed on State Highway 114. Lowe was a very tall man and was known to everyone as "Shorty."

The Davis house at 721 West College Street was built in 1935 for widowed Hattie Davis and her young children. The facade of this house reflects a Tudor Revival influence. Three generations of the Davis family—Hattie, her parents, and her children—have resided on this property, the last being her daughter Inez (née Davis) and her husband, Harlan L. Jewett.

Married in 1877, when she was 15 and he was 17, Martha "Mattie" Brandenburg and John Randolph Willingham eventually owned 545 acres of farmland east of Grapevine. In 1915, they purchased a lot with a 1,600-square-foot house (above) on Main Street. Willingham sold the house, which had been built near the end of the Civil War, and it was moved to 504 West College Street. This relocated house, now called the Terrill-Payne-Fuller House after its occupants through the years, is the second-oldest house in Grapevine. The Willinghams then constructed a new home (below) on their lot and lived there until their deaths. This house was later moved around 1956 to the Bellaire Addition to make way for the construction of a grocery store, which today has been replaced by new retail buildings.

Originally located at 405 South Church Street and later moved to 211 West Franklin Street, this Victorian Queen Anne home was constructed for Daisy Foust (née Huitt) and John Edward Foust in 1910. He owned a mercantile and funeral business at 334 South Main Street. The family business was later named J. E. Foust and Son, when his son John Edward Foust II joined him.

Effie Wright (née Chambers) and Jesse Horn Wright moved to Grapevine in 1926 and later purchased 4 acres of land at 601 West Wall Street, which included a cotton gin and this 1900s Folk Victorian house called the "Ginner's House." The grandchildren remember sleeping under the big oak tree in front of the house in the summertime and in front of the fireplace in the winter. The Joe L. Wright family still owns the property.

The Victorian-style house built in 1898 by Elizabeth Virginia "Jennie" Yancy (née Nash) and Henry Hiram Yancy is located at 1321 West Wall Street. The Yancy farm adjoined the farm belonging to her parents, Elizabeth Nash (née Mouser) and Thomas Jefferson Nash.

A departure from its early-20th-century neighbors, this Austin stone ranch-style house built for Edna Maude Deacon (née Fuller) and William Douglas Deacon was the third house on the lot at 304 East College Street. Built in 1950, this post–World War II era construction was very utilitarian in nature. When the Deacons moved to town due to the gasoline shortage during World War II, they lived in a smaller house on this lot once owned by Annie Moore Trice. This was the site of the Grapevine College dormitory.

The sign in the front yard of this home at 303 Ridge Road, built in 1962, says it all: "Welcome to the most planted acre in Texas. Tours available upon request." Edith Marie Hendrix and Edgar Lee Pewitt were married in 1945 and moved to Grapevine in 1950, where Ed worked with the Soil Conservation Service. Because of his horticulture knowledge, he became known as "Mr. Tree." Edith and Ed have generously given time, money, information, and inspiration to the community of Grapevine.

Dr. Edgar Lee Lancaster and his wife, Dr. Minnie Lee Lancaster (née Schaedel), came to Grapevine in 1953 and opened the first hospital. They developed the Ridgecrest Addition and, in 1966, built this home at 305 Azalea Drive for their family of seven. The Lancasters contributed to the Grapevine community as leaders in the medical field, the United Methodist Church, the Boy Scouts, and other civic organizations.

Judge James Tracy Morehead, credited with naming the town "Grape Vine," built this dogtrot cabin in 1854. Richard Montgomery Gano, a doctor, minister, and Confederate general, purchased the property around 1860. John S. Saunders bought the property in 1879, and his family owned it until 1948. Years later, a member of the Saunders family was looking for it at the original site and discovered it had been moved in 1974 to Old City Park in Dallas and restored. It soon became called "The House That Got Lost."

The Bannister High-Performance House at 424 Ball Street is one of the most energy-efficient houses in Texas as well as the nation, yet the home might be mistaken for one of Grapevine's earliest. Modeled after a c. 1900 Folk Vernacular farmhouse, this home built in 2007 has received numerous national awards. It is a demonstration project for the U.S. Department of Energy's "Building America" program.

Five

COMMUNITY
NEIGHBORS HELPING NEIGHBORS

As settlers arrived on the Grape Vine Prairie, their first concern after lodging was to build churches and schools. Life was hard, and in their struggles they turned to their faith for strength and to education for the betterment of the future generation. John Allen Freeman, a Baptist minister who came to the area in 1845, wrote in his diary about his first sermon here: "The thought we tried to impress upon the minds of God's children was, that He who had heard their prayers in other days, was able to hear them now, and to shield them from every foe, both seen and unseen." He described the worship service as one with "singing of good songs . . . and many shed tears at the end of the service." Pictured above around 1908 is a portion of the residential district of Grapevine, which shows houses, a church (top left), and the Grapevine College and dorm (top center).

A Methodist congregation was chartered in 1865, and the first building was constructed in 1873 on land donated by Rev. E. Nathan Hudgins. Until this structure was built, Hudgins held worship services and prayer meetings in the homes of residents. A larger church (left) was built in 1901 and, as the congregation grew, new sanctuaries were built in 1935 (inset), 1966, and 2002.

Baptists began meeting in homes as early as 1846. Pioneer Baptists began worshiping together in a log cabin schoolhouse across from where the Grapevine Cemetery is today. In 1869, the church was organized and, in 1870, the congregation purchased land on Wall and Church Streets. In 1871, they moved into a new brick building with doors, windows, and no floor. The second church (above) was constructed on Texas Street in 1905 on land donated by Eliza Harriet Morehead (née Jenkins) and Jacob Lyon Morehead. As the church has grown, facilities have been added. In 2009, a site for a new building was purchased in South Grapevine.

Organized around 1880, the Church of Christ constructed its first building (right) in 1884. Most of the members were relatives of Dr. Dabney Minor Lipscomb of whom it was said, "His whole heart seemed engrossed in (the congregation's) true spiritual growth." After it burned to the ground in 1909, another building was constructed on the site at 416 East College Street. The congregation relocated to Park Boulevard in the early 1980s.

The Grapevine Congregation Presbyterian Church, U.S.A., was organized in April 1908 and dissolved in May 1934 because many members had left or died and "it was no longer possible to maintain a church service." In 1951, the First Presbyterian Church (above) was organized and dedicated this small frame building in 1952. Growth of the church called for future expansion. In 1981, a new facility was dedicated on Park Boulevard. Dr. Ira E. Woods, one of Grapevine's mayors, contributed a sizeable memorial to his wife for the purchase of a pipe organ.

Saint Francis of Assisi Catholic Church began in 1949. The Catholic Extension Society and founding members gave money, as well as sponsored a supper, bingo, and cakewalk to purchase the property. Before the church was built, mass was held at the McDonald and Millican homes. The parish doubled in size between 1980 and 1985. A new facility was built in 1985 on Wildwood Lane and has since added more space.

Mount Horuhm Missionary Baptist Church, founded in 1905, is said to be the first African American church between Fort Worth and Denton. It was disbanded, and a landmark on West Wall Street shows its original site. The Love Chapel Church of God in Christ (above) was organized in 1930 with members of 11 African American families forming the first church body. Purchased in 1942, the church property on Turner Street has stood as a cornerstone for nearly 70 years in Grapevine's African American community known as "The Hill." In 2009, the Grapevine Heritage Foundation designated the original site as a historic landmark after the congregation moved to a facility on Dooley Street in 2001.

The historic Grapevine Cemetery was built in 1878 and has been in continuous use since then. It is the resting place of the majority of the town's early business and civic leaders and other citizens, some of whom were veterans of the Civil War, World War I, and World War II. The archway and fencing (above) were a gift from the Bayview Club in celebration of the club's 80th anniversary. The Bayview Club is the oldest study group in Grapevine.

This private family cemetery at Nash Farm is typical of those found around the Grape Vine Prairie area. The pioneer families would often bury their dead on their own properties and mark the graves with native sandstone, which has resulted in many of the grave sites being lost. Other graveyards were founded next to churches. This tombstone at Nash Farm marks the graves of two baby boys.

The early settlers on the Grape Vine Prairie stressed the importance of education and quickly established schools to fulfill the need. By July 1846, there was a log schoolhouse located "in the timbers." In 1868, the Grapevine Masonic Lodge began building the first schoolhouse, and the Grapevine Masonic Institute opened in 1869. In 1886, Prof. J. S. Brown bought the Masonic buildings and began operating the Grapevine College, shown above. The college not only served local young people of all ages but also attracted students from other communities.

The first Grapevine public school was a two-story white frame structure located near College and Church Streets. In 1906, the Grapevine College building was purchased by the public school system. When the two-story redbrick school was erected in 1908 at Worth and Austin Streets, with its two stairways and hall in the middle, the whole community was extremely proud. The high school graduated its first class of one student that year. The large iron bell on top of the building rang every morning, calling the students to school.

In 1938, Central Elementary School (above) was constructed on Austin Street. In 1952, a new high school was constructed on East Worth Street, and land was purchased to the south next to the railroad tracks for a football field and a field house. In 1969, a new high school and stadium were constructed on State Highway 26. The older building housed the junior high. It is now the home of Faith Christian Academy, a private school. Today the public school system is comprised of 19 schools located in Grapevine and Colleyville.

The first African American elementary school was located near Wall and Scribner Streets. Because of the influx of African American families during construction of the Grapevine Dam and Reservoir and the efforts of principal William E. Washington Sr., the new brick Turner Elementary School was built in the 1950s in the African American community of about 15 to 20 families known as "The Hill." Washington came to Grapevine in the early 1950s and worked to modernize the school, started plays and musicals, and conducted commencement ceremonies. The school, located just north of Northwest Highway, was named for one of its teachers, Opal Turner.

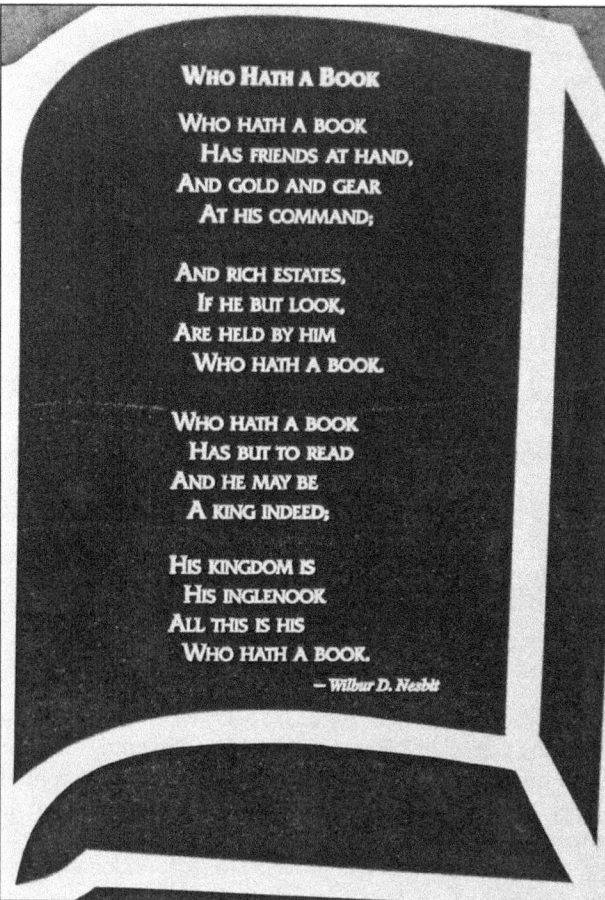

WHO HATH A BOOK

WHO HATH A BOOK
HAS FRIENDS AT HAND,
AND GOLD AND GEAR
AT HIS COMMAND;

AND RICH ESTATES,
IF HE BUT LOOK,
ARE HELD BY HIM
WHO HATH A BOOK.

WHO HATH A BOOK
HAS BUT TO READ
AND HE MAY BE
A KING INDEED;

HIS KINGDOM IS
HIS INGLENOOK
ALL THIS IS HIS
WHO HATH A BOOK.

— *Wilbur D. Nesbit*

After the community had established schools, another public service needed was a local library. The Tarrant County Free Library was organized in 1922, and the first library in Grapevine opened in March 1923 in the front corner of the Farmer's National Bank on Main Street. Today the Grapevine Public Library, built in 1986 at 1201 Municipal Way and enlarged in 2001, is a first-class city-run facility offering more than 200,000 volumes of books, tapes, and programs for the community. The poem, "Who Hath A Book," written by Wilbur Nesbit, was used as the inspiration and title of the sculpture in front of the library. The sculpture was dedicated in November 2001 in honor of past and present librarians and library board members.

An old house became the location of the Grapevine Clinic and Hospital that opened in 1954 at 1011 Northwest Highway. A husband and wife team, Dr. Ed and Dr. Minnie Lee Lancaster moved to the community in 1953 and established and operated the six-bed clinic, which was open 24 hours a day for emergencies, general medical care, low-risk surgeries, and obstetrics.

In 1967, the Grapevine Memorial Hospital and Clinic opened on West College Street as a 30,000-square-foot facility. A foundation begun by Dr. Ed and Dr. Minnie Lee Lancaster and Dr. Carlton and Wanda Pittard owned and operated the new 25-bed facility. In 1981, the hospital merged with Baylor Medical Center. Over the years, it has been expanded to 197 beds, with a new 2003 wing called the Ed and Minnie Lee Lancaster Patient Tower. In 2004, the hospital was renamed the Baylor Regional Medical Center. It is an outstanding facility that has national recognition for its quality medical care.

The Grapevine Volunteer Fire Department is pictured in uniform around 1950. From left to right are (first row) C. E. "Sparky" Himes, O. J. "Buddy" Carlile, Jack Hodges, A. B. Allen, H. D. "Cotton" Thompson, Ed Davis, C. W. "Bill" VanDeventer; (second row) Lumas McPherson, L. T. "Skinny" Lemons, J. C. "Jake" Greener, Laura Faye Berry (the department "mother"), fire chief Charlie Thomas, Dalton Berry, J. Lloyd Fuller, and Harold Lowe.

In 1978, J. C. "Jake" Greener, the first paid fire chief hired by the City of Grapevine, stood beside the 1928 fire truck in front of the fire station. The Grapevine Fire Department got its start in May 1907, when the city council appointed a fire chief and 13 volunteer members of the "Bucket Brigade." Chartered in 1921, it has grown to become a highly acclaimed team of dedicated professional firefighters, with five fire stations and over 100 people serving the Grapevine area.

On February 12, 1907, William Madison Bennett was named the first town marshal. Then in 1909, W. T. Bigby was authorized to construct the jail, called the Calaboose, and to spend $4.50 for the purchase of a set of handcuffs. In contrast, today the modern Grapevine Police and Courts Building houses the police department, 911 center, jail, and municipal court with 93 police officers and 132 employees.

Officer Darren Glenn Medlin was the first Grapevine police officer killed in the line of duty. Pictured is a bronze relief cast of his badge no. 85. He was struck and killed by a drunk driver on an early morning in June 2004 while conducting a traffic stop on State Highway 121. He lived a life consistent with the Latin words, "Sine Cera," denoting honesty and sincerity, found on his Grapevine Police shoulder patch.

The Senior Activities Center at 421 Church Street has been the gathering place for Grapevine's senior citizens since 1978. A wide variety of activities, services, and educational programs are available at the beautiful expanded facility. Participation is open to all senior citizens 55 and over.

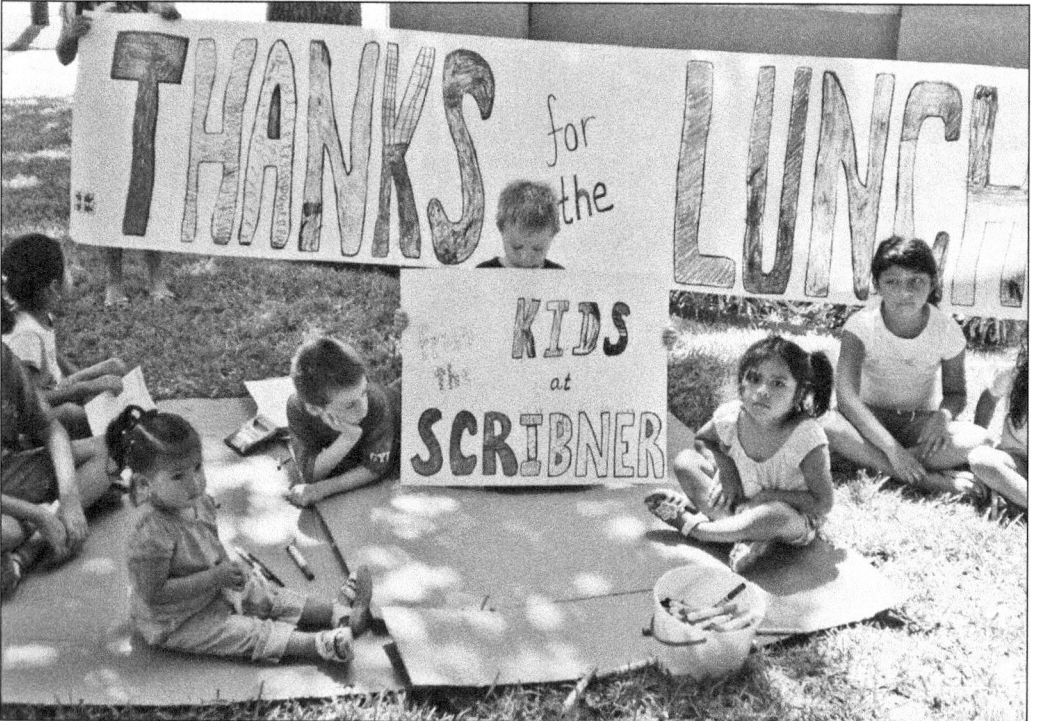

The Grapevine Relief and Community Exchange (GRACE) began in 1987 as a joint outreach of nine local churches and representatives from cities, schools, and local civic organizations. "In the spirit of God's grace, GRACE provides vital necessities for people who are struggling through difficult times," as quoted from their mission statement. By partnering with other organizations, GRACE operates one of the largest civic and nondenominational ecumenical projects in North Texas.

Six

FUN
SOMETHING FOR EVERYONE

In 1998, the Grapevine City Council approved a master plan to insure the development and management of Grapevine's parks, recreation facilities, and open spaces. Oak Grove Park Field Complex opened May 2, 2009, with more than 4,000 local citizens and children attending. Archie St. Clair, artist-in-residence, unveiled his bronze sculpture of three children playing baseball. This opening marked a milestone event for the city in increased recreational opportunities.

Grapevine's first organized baseball team poses for a team picture in 1907. The players, sons of early settlers, were known as the "Grapevine Browns." They traveled to and from the games in a wagon and usually spent the night before returning home.

In the early 1950s, James Richard "Jim" Armstrong, Allen John "A. J." Harper, William Henry "Bill" Yancey, and others organized a Grapevine Little League baseball team. The 1957 Grapevine-area all-star team was, from left to right, (first row) Jerry Gremminger, Gary Bone, Jimmy Hubbard, Tim Harper, John Turner, and John Agnew; (second row) Truman Read, Mike Vester, Jerry Warren, unidentified, Larry Lee, David Roach, Doug Emery, and Donny Kaker.

The Grapevine Botanical Gardens at Heritage Park, at 411 Ball Street, is a beautiful treasure in the heart of historic Grapevine. Established in 2000, it has hundreds of different species of plants, a garden court, walks, benches, and the Ed and Edith Pewitt Outdoor Educational Pavilion. The sculpture *New Season* (right), by Gary Price, was relocated there in 2002. Celebrating Grapevine's position on the migration path of the monarch butterfly between Canada and Mexico, it shows a boy assisting a young girl with a butterfly release. Each year in October, Grapevine celebrates this migration with a Butterfly Flutterby and Gossamer Parade. Pictured below are children in costumes watching as live butterflies are released.

Benjamin Richard Wall made a trip to New York around 1913 and secured a legacy for all boys of Grapevine: the No. 7 Boy Scout Unit Charter, the first chartered troop west of the Mississippi. Pictured in the 1950s is Boy Scout Troop 7 canoeing on Lake Grapevine, which offered many opportunities for the scouts to work on their different badges.

As two fishermen try their hand at catching fish in Lake Grapevine, three boys jump from the pier near the boat docks. The lake was built in 1952 to provide drinking water as well as to help with flood control. It has become a major source of recreation for the area.

Lake Grapevine attracts over one million visitors each year who enjoy sailing, fishing, boating, camping, and picnicking on the beaches. Two golf courses, Grapevine Golf Course and Cowboys Golf Club, have been developed on the land below the dam. In the background are the Glass Cactus and the Gaylord Texan Resort and Convention Center on Lake Grapevine.

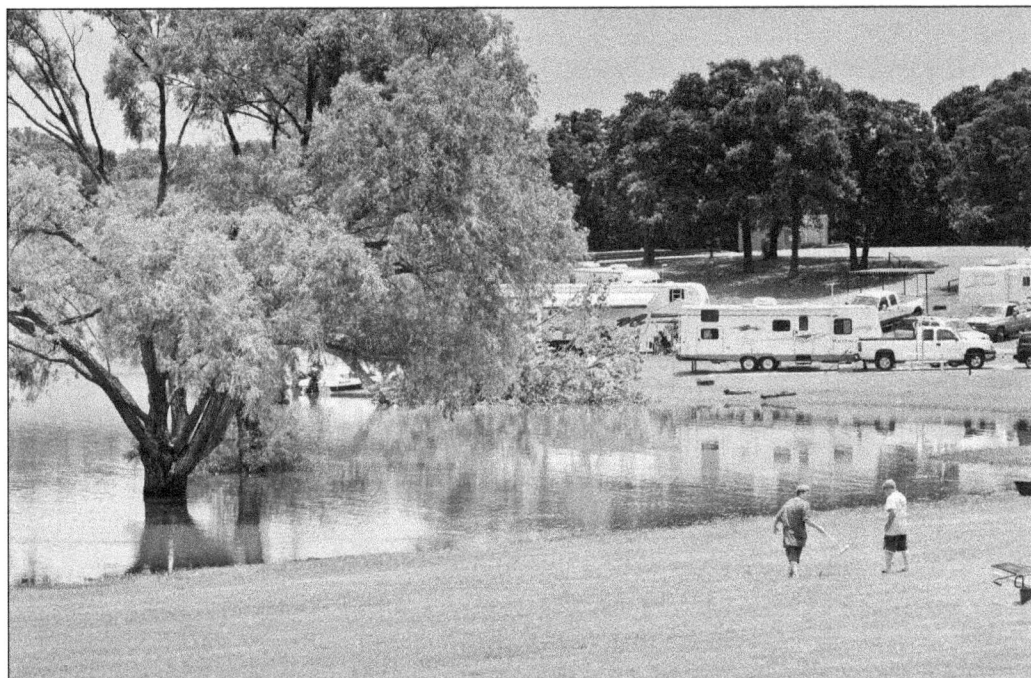

Camping at Lake Grapevine can be primitive or comfortable with modern conveniences. There are camping spots for tents, RVs, and cabins. Wooded areas and trails for exploring, waterfront views, playgrounds, boat ramps, and courtesy docks abound.

Some children had very little time for play in the early 1900s. At left, Clifton Duke, on the tricycle, and his sister Mable took a break from their chores in 1914. Their mother died when they were young and both worked hard on their grandparents' farm, often picking cotton until their fingers bled. In contrast to the simple tricycle on a dirt patch in front of the house, bicycle riders, hikers, and joggers today have an elaborate trail system throughout Grapevine. Bud Sheley is shown below enjoying his sport of bicycling along one of the many trails near Lake Grapevine.

Because Grapevine did not have a golf course in the 1960s, avid golfers purchased the old hearse (above) from Lucas Funeral Home for their out-of-town excursions. In order to have room for their golf clubs, some of the group, Harlan Jewett, W. D. "Ted" Willhoite, Allen John "A. J." Harper, and William Henry "Bill" Yancey, built a wooden box with the sign, "Golfer's Special," for the top. Today Grapevine Men's Golf Association holds the A. J. Harper Memorial Golf Tournament to honor his passion for the game and his efforts in establishing the Grapevine Golf Course in 1979. Pictured below at the golf course are, from left to right, Harper's descendants and several members of the original "Hearse Gang": Gregory Rains Harper, Stephanie Harper Lucke, Brian Timothy Harper, Harlan Jewett, Marvin Timothy "Tim" Harper, T. William Dickey, Travis Matthews, and Billy Alvin "Bill" Powers. Today Grapevine has another golf course, the Cowboys Golf Club, which is the world's first NFL-themed golf course, paying tribute to the Dallas Cowboys.

The Grapevine Community Activities Center at 1175 Municipal Way, open to all Grapevine residents and business owners, recently celebrated its 10th anniversary. It boasts a wide variety of entertaining activities for all ages, with a fitness room, two full-sized gyms, two racquetball courts, an indoor track, and game room. Yoga, art, dance, and cooking classes are just a few of the activities available, and they all spell fun.

Seven

FRIENDS
BE OUR GUESTS

Friends and business people gathered to have a soda in 1948 at City Drug on Main Street. It was originally called the Olympia Confectionery and owned by Clarence Emory "Pie" Stewart and later Clifford Jenkins Wall. Roy Chambers purchased it in 1947 and named it the City Drug. In its early years, Grapevine had family-owned establishments that offered intimate settings for friends as well as travelers to enjoy a soda or a meal. The locally owned hotels/motels offered lodging for its out-of-town guests.

Millican's Café was owned and operated by Nellie Juanita Millican (née Andrews) and her husband, Clarence Franklin Millican, a very large man. Nellie was an extremely good cook, noted for her homemade pies. For the dedication ceremony of the Northwest Highway in 1932, the community selected the tallest, smallest, and stoutest Grapevine citizens. Clarence Millican was chosen the stoutest, and he can be seen in a picture of the three contest winners in the Grapevine Historical Museum.

John Starr and John Lemmons owned a restaurant on Main Street north of Willhoite's Garage. Photographed around 1920, they stand ready for customers.

A popular trend in Grapevine today is "adaptive reuse" of buildings, giving historic structures new uses and new lives. Pictured above is the building at 124 East Worth Street, used from 1935 to 1973 by the Lucas Funeral Home, whose history goes back to Lucas descendants in 1860. J. T. Lucas owned it from 1947 until his death in 1970. Today it is Esparza's Restaurante Mexico, a popular dinner rendezvous. Located next door at 116 East Worth Street is a sports bar called Lazy Bones Neighborhood Sports Grill and Pub, shown below. The building was constructed in 1916 and was originally the William Cameron and Company Lumberyard.

Phillip Ray "Phil" Parker opened Wilhoitte's Restaurant in 1981 at 432 South Main Street. Phil's grandfather and father, Luther Walter Parker and Luther Walter "L. W." Parker Jr., once owned Parker Appliance and Furniture Store on Main Street. Phil, proud of his Grapevine heritage and wanting to preserve an important part of Grapevine's history, purchased and renovated Willhoite's Garage and carried forward the Willhoite name. He and his family have made Willhoite's Restaurant into another Main Street icon. Pictured at left is John Mayfield, manager, standing in front of the 1927 Model T, which sits on an automobile lift and serves as the focal point of the buffet, reminding visitors of the building's original use.

The old buildings on Main Street have been restored to their natural beauty and offer space for retail businesses. Several of the restaurants now have sidewalk patio service, and people enjoy relaxing outdoors while dining and shopping.

Wineries in Grapevine are a successful new venture for the business community. Homestead Winery and Tasting Room, an eclectic winery that serves only Texas wine, is in the restored Wingate Hezekiah "Wink" Lucas II Folk Victorian house at 211 East Worth Street. In the 1880s, Lucas and his brother Dave Lucas co-owned the General Mercantile Business on Main Street that led the Lucas family into the funeral business. Penny and Don Bigbie, owners of Cross Timbers Winery (below) restored the Dorris/Brock home and rebuilt the barn at 805 North Main Street. Wine tasting is offered in the main house, and the barn, replicated in 2001, is used as a rental facility for special events. Dr. W. E. Dorris, who came to Grapevine in 1871 and was the father of Dr. Thomas Benton Dorris, is believed to have been the original owner. John W. Brock purchased the house in 1908. Both wineries commemorate the past while celebrating the present.

In 1857, Eli Mathis Jenkins opened the only general merchandise business in Grapevine. It was subsequently owned and operated by Jenkins' son-in-law Junius Edward Merritt "June" Yates and known as Yates Dry Goods Store. It was passed through the family and continued in operation for 128 years. In 1890, Jenkins's 12-year old grandson Earl Yates Sr. became a full-time employee. Lemual Haven "L. H." Cook (center) and Ernest E. "Shorty" Lowe (back right) worked there around 1920. A glass case at the Grapevine Historical Museum displays early-to-mid-1900s items from Yates Dry Goods Store.

The E. J. Lipscomb and Son Dry Goods Store at 414 South Main Street was owned and operated by Edward Jenner Lipscomb and/or his son Huber from 1909 until 1967. Pictured above waiting for customers are Judie Byas Forbes Martin, affectionately called "Miss Judie" by customers, and the owner, Huber Lipscomb.

Shopping on Main Street in Grapevine today (at right) is quite different from yesteryear, with its many sophisticated stores and goods available to customers. Yet it remains the same, with locally owned businesses and small-town friendly service. Also available for the prudent shopper to explore is the 1.6 million square feet of discount shopping at Grapevine Mills Mall (below). Opened in 1997 at 3000 Grapevine Mills Parkway, it offers hundreds of the best names in retail outlet stores.

Grapevine's Baker Hotel (above) was a three-story wooden structure on Main Street with 15 rooms and one bathroom, built around the 1870s and moved to Worth Street in 1912. The hotel was a busy place, especially when the railroad came to Grapevine, bringing traveling salesmen. Many interesting stories abound about the old hotel. One elderly gentleman who was drinking too much shot his nagging wife to death with a shotgun. Barton Starr, Grapevine's first mayor, was called to the scene and later said they were a nice couple, except for his drinking. The Baker Hotel was torn down in 1965. The Wallis Hotel (below), erected in 1891 near the railroad depot at the corner of Main and Hudgins Streets, also served travelers and salesmen. Unfortunately the hotel, a beautiful brick building, was not a financial success and was torn down in 1931.

In 1946, W. D. "Bud" Guest built the Grapevine Motel Plaza on Northwest Highway and Starnes Street out of recycled lumber from army barracks. Lovey Davis Buckner Yates and her husband, Estill "Bud" Yates, owned the Palace Theatre and, in 1947, they agreed to exchange properties. The Yates operated the motel until 1968 when they retired.

Built in 1995, the Garden Manor Bed and Breakfast at 205 East College Street looks historic due to its careful construction and adherence to the City of Grapevine's design guidelines for the College Street Historic District. Garden Manor is the only bed and breakfast in Northeast Tarrant County and the only lodging in Grapevine's historic district.

Grapevine's city leaders in the 1980s and 1990s realized the treasure of the Grape Vine Prairie in much the same way as the first pioneers and knew Grapevine was destined to be a unique, historic "prairie town." Taking advantage of the Dallas-Fort Worth International Airport's close proximity and the recreational amenities at Lake Grapevine, these visionaries sought and landed some mighty big fish. The Gaylord Texan Resort and Convention Center (above) chose to locate on Lake Grapevine at 1501 Gaylord Trail. It has 1,511 guest rooms and 400,000 square feet of flexible meeting spaces to provide authentic Texas hospitality. With its 4-plus acres of indoor gardens and winding waterways, the Gaylord serves as a lodging, dining, and shopping mecca for out-of-town guests and locals, too. Across Highway 26, is the Great Wolf Lodge Waterpark and Resort (below) at 100 Great Wolf Drive. Their indoor water parks—and some cute howling wolves—invite families to enjoy its rustic elegance.

Eight

CELEBRATION
COMING TOGETHER

The people of Grapevine have always enjoyed celebrating together with events, parades, and festivals, whether it is for a holiday or simply a reason to gather. In a 1921 parade, Edward Thomas "Ed" Simmons drove this wagon with his son James Edward "Hugh" Simmons, sitting on a tethered pony on the wagon bed. Simmons was advertising Purina Feeds for the feed store.

A "womanless wedding" was a popular event for many years and always drew a crowd in Grapevine. This "wedding" took place April 12, 1917, and not only did everyone have fun, they also raised money for the Red Cross. Advertisements for local businesses can be seen across the top of the stage.

For seven years, from 1935 to 1941, cantaloupes were king, and Grapevine celebrated the annual Cantaloupe Festival and crowned the Cantaloupe Queen. At one time, 25,000 acres of cantaloupes were planted in the Grapevine area, and in 1935, at least 100 truckloads of melons were brought into town. In 1939, Jessie Lou Hall Nelson perched on top of a load of her father's cantaloupes ready to take part in the festivities.

A good reason for the farmers to come to town in 1930 was to see a farm truck rally and demonstration (above). Around 1950, citizens gather on Main Street for a parade (below). High school baton twirlers are at the far left of the picture, and the Tate Hardware Store sign is across the top of the building. The mule-drawn cart is advertising Austin Patio Ranch, created by Pat and Clyde Stinson, a party facility with an exciting Western theme. This historic dude ranch is still located near the Grapevine Mills Mall and is currently owned by the Hilton DFW Lakes Hotel.

The homecoming parade and football game always drew big crowds. This photograph taken in 1954 shows the homecoming queen and her attendants riding down Main Street on a decorated float. In the background, the sign on the building cites the Parker Furniture and Appliance Store, owned by the Luther Walker Parker family.

Celebrations occur in Grapevine all year, but none is quite as special as those around Christmas. The Grapevine High School band is pictured as they march past the Palace Theatre in one of the annual Christmas Parades of Lights, the largest lighted Christmas parade in North Texas.

The Gazebo downtown is appropriately decorated for each holiday and event in Grapevine. At Christmas, the Gazebo, along with a 35-foot community Christmas tree, is decked out with twinkling lights choreographed to Christmas music and is called the Christmas Light Show Spectacular. Grapevine is now trademarked as the "Christmas Capital of Texas."

In the spirit of the Christmas holiday, the Gaylord Texan Resort and Convention Center on Lake Grapevine hosts a holiday spectacular called ICE! In 2009, its fifth year to host the event, the resort brought 40 master artisans from Harbin, China, to carve two million pounds of ice in 30 days, creating awe-inspiring sculptures, such as the nativity scene pictured.

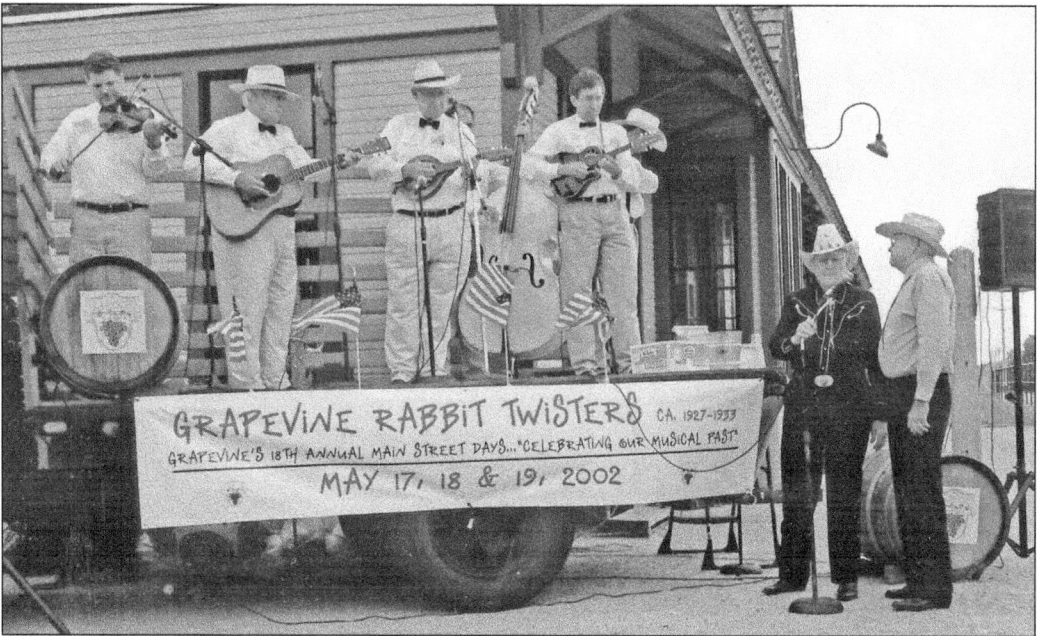

A popular form of entertainment in the 1920s and 1930s was the fiddle band, which consisted of a very good fiddler and backup musicians playing mandolin, guitar, bass fiddle, and perhaps the piano. The Rabbit Twisters were one of the best known in the area and played for square dances and parties and even had a regular show on the WFAA radio for a time. In 2002, at the annual Main Street Days Celebration, contemporary musicians portrayed the original Grapevine Rabbit Twisters, while brothers James B. "J. B." and Charles Wilfred "Bill" VanDeventer, whose father was a part of the original group, sang for the audience. Below, another accomplished fiddle band, the Coon Hunters, played live in the WFAA radio studio. Members were, from left to right, Carl Long, Carl Connely, Alonzo Biggers, and John Henry McPherson.

The Palace Arts Center is comprised of the Palace Theatre and the Lancaster Theatre, two Main Street buildings that have been restored and connected. The Palace Theatre was the place to see movies for nearly 30 years after opening in 1940. Its original design has been restored through the preservation work of the Grapevine Heritage Foundation (GHF). The GHF board is shown beneath the restored marquee (at right). The Palace Theatre hosts many special events, movies, and different entertainment programs all year, but its claim to fame is the Grapevine Opry, which began in January 1975. Since 1987, Rocky Gribble has produced the high-quality, family-friendly country music show that packs the house every Saturday night.

The annual spring event hosted by the Grapevine Heritage Foundation at the restored Nash Farm is appropriately called "Spring into Nash Farm." There are many family activities for all to learn about life on the farm (above). Adults and children can play games, ride ponies, meet farm animals (below), milk a goat, take a tractor ride, or plant a garden. Teaching events, such as weaving and cooking as well as seasonal activities, are offered monthly.

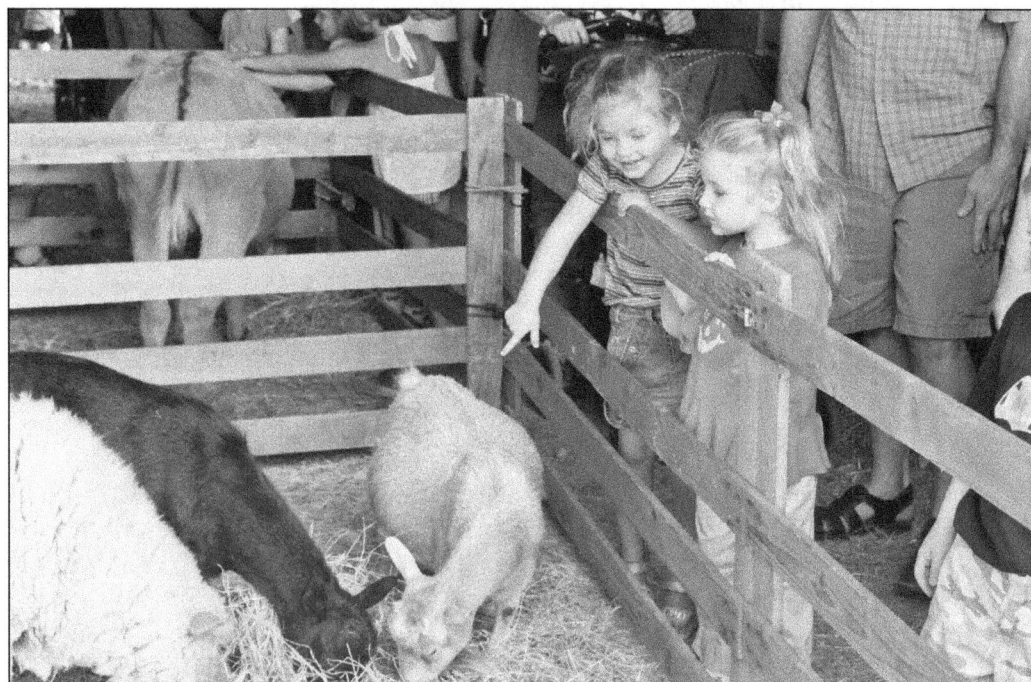

To help generate financial support for preservation projects, the Grapevine Convention and Visitors Bureau presents two annual major downtown festivals, Main Street Outdoor Adventure in May and GrapeFest in September. Both events feature vendors for great shopping, a carnival for the kids, live music, and delicious food. GrapeFest is the largest wine festival in the Southwest, with Texas wines being its focus. Pictured at right is Grapevine's historic Main Street flooded with guests enjoying the sights and sounds, as the *Grapevine Nightwatchman* atop city hall stands as a sentinel above the festivities. Pictured below, GrapeFest visitors have a "grape stomping good time."

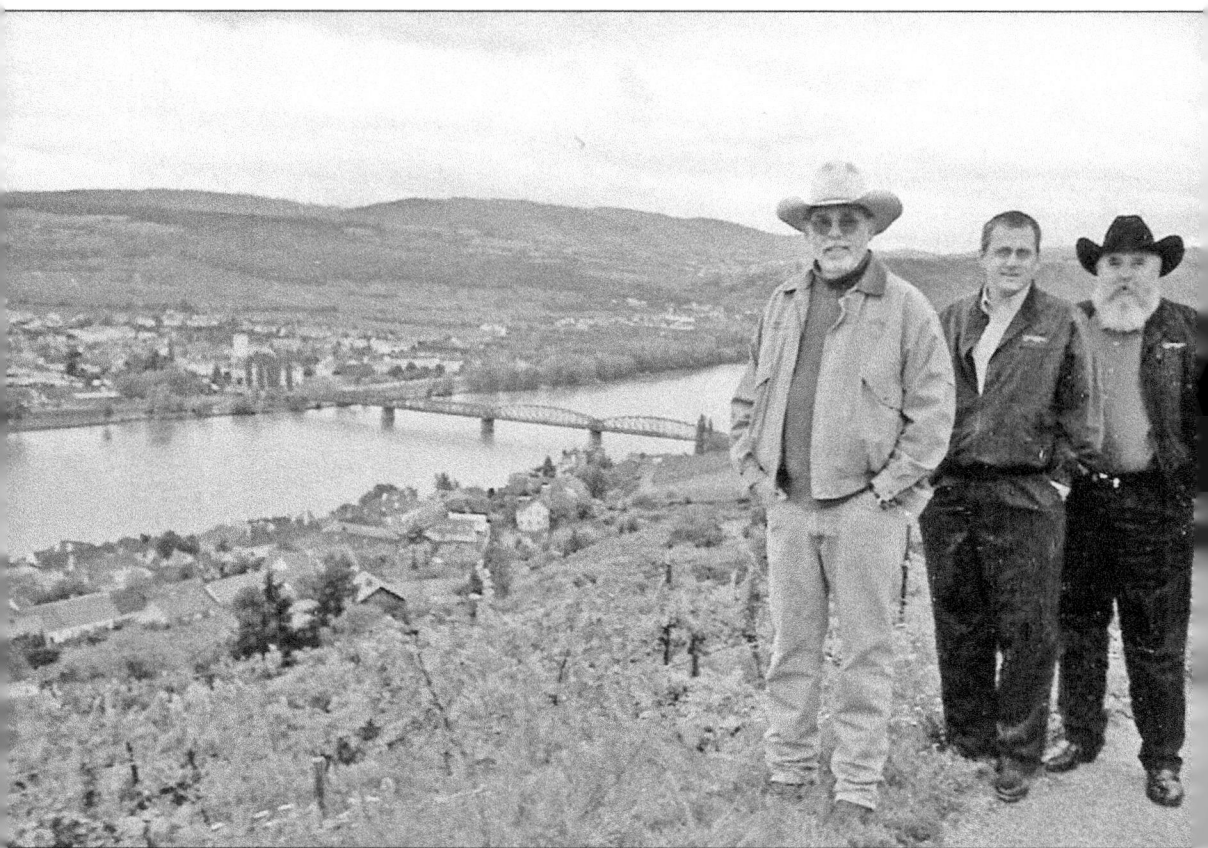

Grapevine's storied past and the progressive thinking of its city leaders to preserve that past have caused it to rank among the most fascinating places to visit in Texas. Two of the most influential of those enterprising leaders are Mayor William D. Tate (left) and Paul W. McCallum (right), executive director of the Grapevine Convention and Visitors Bureau. They are standing in the vineyard overlooking Krems, Austria, beside the Danube River. Krems participates with Grapevine in the Sister City Program, along with Parras de la Fuente, Mexico, and West Lothian, Scotland. The purpose of the program is to exchange knowledge in areas of history, culture, the arts, science, and technology.

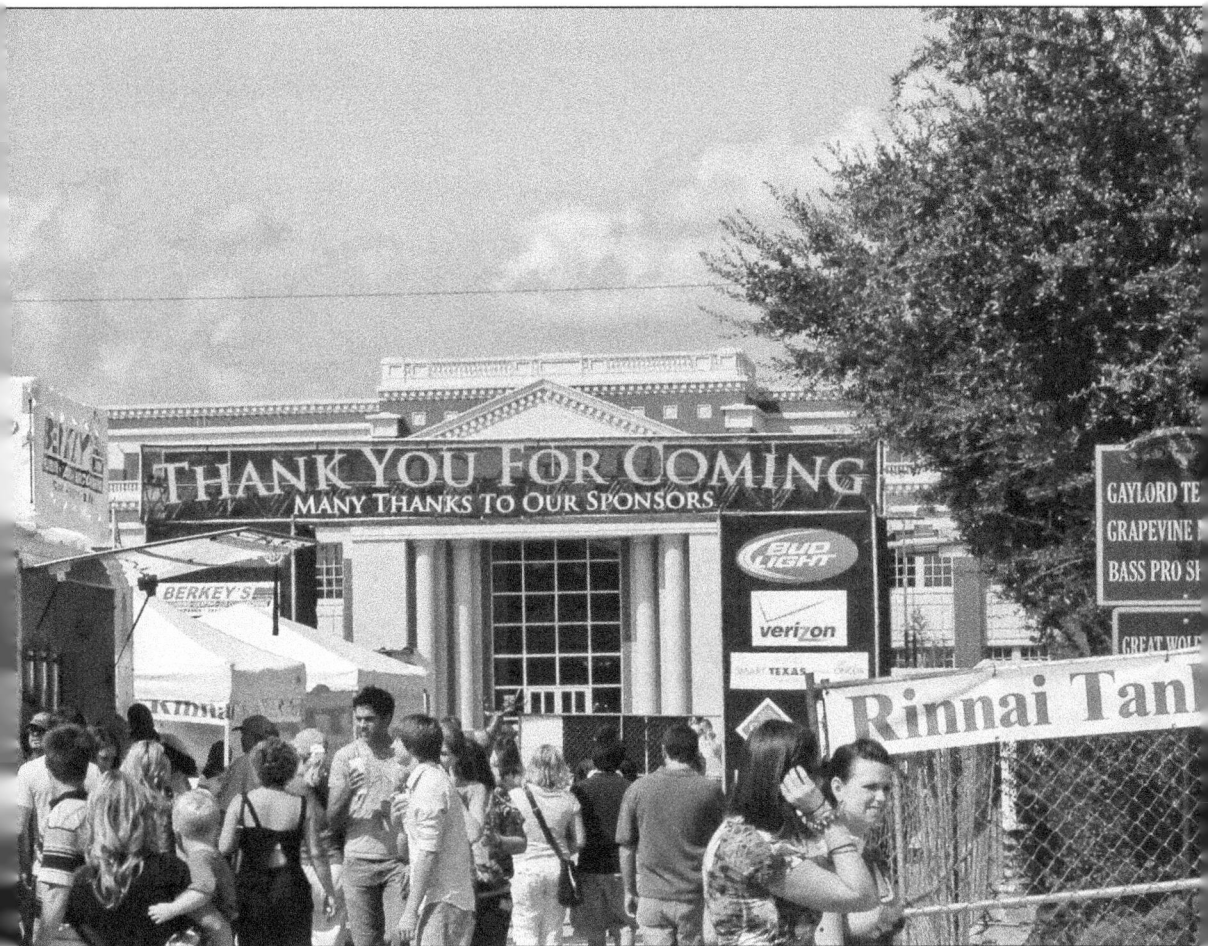

This sign says it all. Grapevine, nestled between Dallas and Fort Worth, provides charm and escape from the big cities, with its historic Main Street and museums, restored homes and farm, vintage train, festivals, wineries, restaurants, hotels, lake activities, and international airport. Welcome to Grapevine, the prairie community that has become a door to the world. Thank you for coming!

Visit us at
arcadiapublishing.com

www.ingramcontent.com/pod-product-compliance
Lightning Source LLC
Chambersburg PA
CBHW050627110426

42813CB00007B/1743

* 9 7 8 1 5 3 1 6 5 6 4 3 0 *